When God Said No

Bob and Lisa Perron

LITTLE RED HOUSE
PUBLISHING

"This is a must read for adopted children as well as those who have adopted children. Being an adopted child myself, I struggle with separation anxiety because there wasn't an understanding of the deep wound one experiences at birth when separated from his or her birth mother. This book is moving and funny and even allows their children to speak and give testimony to what it's like being in an adoptive family. The care and concern Bob and Lisa took to connect each adopted child with their birth families, foster families, and heritage reveals how their faith informed their actions to be empathetic and compassionate to each person who loved these children along the way and to continue to be a part of their lives. This unselfish act of love is how, I believe, God loves us and calls us to love each other. Bob and Lisa have given us their beautiful journey of how God takes what we see as suffering and turns it into joy that is beyond our dreams."

—John Angotti
Adopted child

"If you're anything like me, this book will keep you laughing, move you to tears, and leave you contemplating God's plan for *your* life as well. Open, honest, and real, Bob and Lisa Perron pour their hearts out on paper and take you inside their journey with all of its twists and turns to a God-sized family. A great reminder for everyone that God's ways are perfect, even in the 'noes' and 'not yets.'"
—Danny May
Director of Marriage & Family Life,
Diocese of Owensboro, KY

"Bob and Lisa Perron take you on an inspirational journey from heartbreak to Hallelujah! This book is a must read for families going through infertility."
—Del-Metri Williams

Founder and CEO of Rx Interactive

"Bob and Lisa Perron are wonderful storytellers. As adoptive parents who struggled with infertility in the early part of our marriage, this book hits really close to home. *When God Said No* is heartfelt, encouraging, and simply a beautiful memoir of the Perron family experience. You will laugh. You will cry. You will connect."

—Eric & Becky Groth
Founders, ODB Films
Executive Producers of *Paul: Apostle of Christ*

For Kelsey, Mackenzie, Bobby, Isaiah, and Emma.

Worth the Wait

I prayed and prayed for children,

For years, it seemed, in vain.

My heart overwhelmed with sorrow;

I asked God, "What did I do to deserve this?"

Now the mother of five,

Through both adoption and birth.

My heart overflows with gratitude;

I ask God, "What did I do to deserve this?"

Table of Contents

INTRODUCTION: CATCHING BUBBLES

D o you remember what it was like when you were a child and you really wanted something, I mean, wanted something so much that you thought you couldn't possibly live without it, and when it comes time to ask your parents for this necessary item, they tell you no? Do you remember the disappointment, fury, and the feeling of being misunderstood? After all, if they truly understood how deep your desire was, they couldn't possibly deny it to you—if they loved you, that is.

Everything inside you screamed "Why?!" Sometimes their reasons made sense. Other times, their reasons were difficult to accept. Sometimes they just said the dreaded, "Because I said so." That was the worst. It felt like they were purposely torturing you—that somehow they had broken the trust between you.

The truth is that your parents always had your best interests at heart. Even when you didn't understand the reason they said no, their motivation wasn't to hurt you but to protect you. Or maybe they knew that something better was coming—something that would be far beyond what you currently desired. All you had to do was wait. It's difficult enough to experience this disappointment as a child, but when it happens to you in your adult life, and God is the one telling you no, it's particularly devastating.

As long as I can remember, I have always wanted to have children—lots of children. This desire to be a mother was in my very DNA. It was my purpose—the reason I was created. I knew this was true just as I knew that the sky is blue and water is wet. From the moment Bob and I got married, I felt suspended, just waiting for my dream of having a baby to come true.

But God said no.

My mother asked me once why being a mother was so important to me. I told her that it was the way God made me. When I was knit in my mother's womb, my desire to be a mother was woven into my very being. I didn't voice my next thought to my mother. *And, he abandoned me.* How could a loving God, a loving father, devastate his child so?

As weeks turned into months and months turned into years, my faith and trust in God shattered. It didn't happen all at once, but piece-by-piece, each painful shard cutting as it fell away. I know that I am not the only one to have experienced this. Whenever anyone experiences tragedy, he or she cannot help but ask why. As Christians, we know that God can do anything, can prevent evil things from happening. We just don't understand when he chooses not to—as if knowing the reason would make it easier to accept.

Suffering through infertility was much like trying to catch bubbles. The bubbles were hope for a child. Most months they floated out of reach before we could try and catch one. Other times, as one landed into our hands, it would pop before we could grasp it. When one finally did land in our hands, I couldn't appreciate its beauty. I didn't notice its perfect shape or the iridescent colors that changed as one looks at it from different angles. I couldn't trust that this bubble was the answer to our prayers, the fulfillment of our dreams. It wasn't until we looked into the face of our baby and held her in our arms that we realized that, like our parents' no when we were children, God's no meant *wait*.

This is a story of utter disappointment, eventual acceptance, and tremendous gratitude. Even though our family did not come into being in the manner we had envisioned, it was so much better than we'd ever imagined.

~~DIFFERENT~~ UNIQUE

From Lisa

From an early age, I understood two things about
myself. First, every cell of my body cried out to
be a mother. And second, I wanted to own a bunch of
animals, the more the better. Acquiring pets proved to be
the easier of the two goals. I remember at nine years old
hearing on the news that there was a twelve-year-old
mother. I was much too young to understand the tragedy of
the news story. I just thought to myself, "Only three more
years." I knew nothing about how babies were made, nor
did I understand God's hope for every family. I only knew I
wanted a baby of my own, as soon as possible.

In high school, whenever a teacher or fellow student
would ask me what I wanted to do after I graduated, I
always answered the same: I wanted to stay home and raise
my kids. This disappointed my female teachers especially.
"You could be so much more," they'd say, and I'd reply,
"What could be more important?"

Wanting a big family shouldn't have surprised anyone.
I am the fifth child of six. My only sister is the oldest,
followed by three brothers, then me, and finally my little
brother. When I was born, my sister rode on a bus from
Topeka, Kansas, to Wichita, Kansas, to visit my aunt and
uncle while my mom and I were in the hospital. She was so
happy to finally have a sister, she told everyone on the bus
about me. Teresa was my favorite person in the world. She
never made me feel like I was in the way. She got married
when I was seven, which drastically changed my role at
home.

I have always been my own person, many times
feeling as if I didn't fit anywhere. For much of my life, I
assumed that I was the only one that felt that way. I've
come to realize that it is more rare when a person doesn't
feel like a misfit at least once in a while. I realize now that
this feeling of being different prepared me for life that was
far from ordinary. As much as I dreamed of having a
Waltons kind of family one day, it was not to be.

A couple years ago, I was struck by a childhood
memory, a memory that I hadn't thought about in many
years. I was in the fourth grade, and my family had an
appointment to see a family counselor. I really didn't
understand why we needed to go to this appointment, but
apparently it wasn't optional for me. Recalling this day
back in 1974 brought up emotions that I thought were long

gone. Out of the memory emerged the following poem that illustrates where my feelings of being a stranger wherever I went came from.

The Mirror

The mirror hung on the West wall of the counselor's office
Watching the distribution of roles.
I impatiently waited for my turn.
Role model, Troublemaker, Jock, Brain, and Entertainer,
All taken by my siblings.
"She's never home," my brother said,
Sending me to the corner.
I had my role: Outsider.
I wondered who watched from behind the mirror.
Did they even see me?

My mother cried, my father worried,
Desperate to save their wayward son.
My siblings talked of how they fit in
As Role Model, Troublemaker, Jock, and Brain
While the Entertainer made faces at his reflection.
If he got close enough,
Whom would he see?

I sat on the white tiled floor
And looked longingly at the comfy couch,
Where my family sat without me.

And I wished that I could be
A Role Model, Troublemaker, Jock, Brain, or Entertainer.
I yearned to be all of those things, but I was none.
I looked at the mirror across the room
Even I couldn't see me.

I claimed the mirror as my own,
Holding it in front of me wherever I went.
My siblings looked in my direction
Only seeing the part of me that reflected them.
Role Model, Troublemaker, Jock, Brain, and Entertainer.
I was all of those things and also none.
If they looked close enough,
Would they see me?

I tried to be the Role Model
But no one would follow.
I tried to cause trouble, but it just wasn't me.
Not athletic enough to be the Jock,
Not smart enough to be the Brain,
And too quiet to be the Entertainer.
I tried all those things but succeeded at none.
When would I see me?

At times I laid my mirror aside
To experience life without looking through,
To feel sand between my toes

And smell the salty ocean breeze,
To see my own reflection in the water.
Role Model, Troublemaker, Jock, Brain, and Entertainer,
I was all of those things and also none.
If I got close enough,
Would I actually see me?

I kept ahold of my mirror
And wielded it whenever I returned home.
Going through the motions of hugs
And awkward conversations,
Holding them back and hoping.
All the while reflecting,
The Role Model, Troublemaker, Jock, Brain, and
Entertainer.
I am all of those things and also none.
Will I ever let them close enough to see me?

And now paper is my mirror.
I fill the pages
Full of the words I cannot say.
Reflecting the Role Model, Troublemaker, Jock, Brain, and
Entertainer.
I am all of those things and also none.
If one reads close enough,
That person will see me.

In that room all those years ago, my new identity was created. One, unfortunately that was based on a lie. I was supposed to be the outsider, even in my own family— especially in my own family. It would be decades before I recognized the lie of my role. My family has always embraced my oddness as just a part of who I am. They loved me because of it not in spite of it. I am happy to say that I no longer need the mirror. But, how I wish I hadn't wasted so many years hiding behind it.

The discovery of self is a lifelong journey. We are different people at different seasons of our lives. Just when we think we've got ourselves figured out, something happens that reveals a whole other side to ourselves. I don't think we will fully know who we are until we are face-to-face with our creator.

The day I married my husband Bob, I thought that all of my dreams of motherhood and having a large family were finally coming true. I remember thinking as I stood posing for pictures after the ceremony that this time next year, I'll have a baby. What followed that day was nothing like I had dreamed. Eventually, I would realize that what God had in mind for my husband and me was far more beautiful than any dream I could ever imagine. But, we would have to suffer greatly before we achieved it.

From Bob

When you are the son of an Air Force Airman, your life is constantly on the move. It seems like every year we were packing up and moving to a new base. My early years were filled with great memories of making new friends and seeing new places. You make friends differently when you know that you only have a few months before will you will be saying goodbye to those friends and be off to a new adventure. I am the oldest, which of course meant that I was third in command. I took my role as big brother seriously and remember from an early age feeling like I always had to be in control. I didn't understand this at the time, but it didn't hurt that I am an extreme extrovert. I walk into every situation confident that everyone will like me. I was in my twenties before I had the realization sometimes that is not true. Lisa would probably say that I was in my forties.

As a child, it was easy for me to make friends because everybody else my age was in the same situation. Life on a military base for a kid could be a lot of fun. I remember being able to go out and play all day long. Life on base was a safe place. The way base housing was set up, I had plenty of friends to play with and took full advantage of it.

I remember one time a group of my friends went on a pirate adventure, looking for hidden treasures. The older kids convinced us that the treasure was hidden under a big round metal disc that was located in the middle of an open grassy area. We knew that if we could just open up that disk, the treasure would be ours. We didn't realize then that underneath that sewage manhole was a completely different kind of nugget. Using my great six-year-old understanding of physics, I devised a lever, actually the end of an old broomstick, and we set out to open up the big metal disc. We stuck the broom handle in an opening on the side, and all of my friends and I pushed down on the other end of the broom. Before long, the big round disc had opened up slightly. I said to my friends, "Hold on to the end of the broomstick, and I will open it the rest of the way." I stuck my fingers in the opening and told them to pull the stick out. The next thing I remember was being on my way to the emergency room after the adults had found me, and my fingers, stuck in the manhole. There was no treasure to be found that day, but I'm sure that there was a lesson in there somewhere about not trying to do things on your own.

My need to be in control has been a challenge for me in many areas of my life, including my spiritual life. I think the combination of being the oldest child and growing up as a military brat has made it very difficult for me to just "let go and let God." Don't get me wrong; I took discernment on what God called me to do with my life tremendously seriously. I even went into the seminary, believing that I might be called to the priesthood. When I got married, I was sure that God's plan for me was to be a father of many children. I loved kids and was open to however many God blessed us with.

When I found out that we were not going to be able to have children, it was a crushing blow. Lisa and I definitely dealt with the news differently, but for me it was the ultimate moment of not being in control, and I hated that feeling almost as much as the news that we would not be able to have kids.

LOVE ~~AT FIRST SIGHT~~ EVENTUALLY

From Bob

I love to hear stories about how married couples met. I especially love those stories when a couple meets each other and instantly fall in love. That is not my story. I met Lisa when I was a senior in high school. She was a friend of my little sister, who was a freshman in high school at the time.

Like most seniors, I had no interest in hanging out with my kid sister. She and her friends were annoying. By far her most annoying friend was a noisy, bouncy, freshman cheerleader. Although this girl was naturally a quiet person, when she put on that cheerleader's uniform, she transformed. She was loud, obnoxious, and never seemed to stop talking.

One time after a Friday night football game, I was driving down the main boulevard of our town as the girls jumped up and down in the backseat to the beat of my blaring music. It looked as if I had one of those low-riders that had hydraulic lift kits that looked as if a car was jumping as it glided down the road. The cheerleader rolled down the window in the back seat of my car, sat on the window ledge, and yelled at the top of her lungs, "We're going to Big Cheese and we have a coupon!" (Big Cheese was a pizza place that we would frequent after football games.) All I could think was how much I hoped none of my friends witnessed this embarrassing moment. I could have never imagined in a million years that one day I'd end up marrying that freshman cheerleader.

From Lisa

Our first official date was on Valentine's Day in 1986. Bob took me to one of his favorite Chinese restaurants. The place was packed. When we finally got seated, we ended up sitting at a table in the middle of the room. Normally, I preferred to sit in a booth. In a corner. Where no one would see me. What made this table placement worse was the fact that I had never eaten Chinese food before. I felt as if everyone stared at me while perused the menu without any idea what I was reading. Thankfully, Bob was okay with that and ordered for us both.

Our food was served family style. We had two entrees of who knows what (I think they had chicken. I hope they had chicken.) and a large platter of steamed rice. There I was in the middle of the restaurant, on a first date, clueless on how to eat the food sitting in front of me. Bob waited.

"Go ahead and get your food."

Embarrassed, I said, "I don't know how."

Bob smiled wide and explained to me that you put the entrée on top of the rice. Luckily, he didn't even mention chopsticks. After dinner, we went to see a movie called *Wildcats*, starring Goldie Hawn as a high school football coach, which was the perfect choice of activities for this introvert pushed to the max of my comfort zone.

Before I go further with our story, I need to talk a moment about our personalities. If the terms extrovert and introvert were on each end of a scale where one can place their unique personality somewhere on the spectrum, Bob would be as far to the extrovert side as possible, and I would be on the total opposite side.

In Merriam-Webster's dictionary, an extrovert is described "broadly, a gregarious and unreserved person." An introvert is one who "turn(s) inward in upon itself." In other words, Bob needs people, lots of them, to energize him. I, on the other hand, need alone, quiet time to refuel. This difference in personalities has created some misunderstandings over the years.

For example, Bob processes verbally. When he's considering options, he talks about each one like it's the best option. Many times I would think that he's made a decision, when in fact he's nowhere near a final choice.

I process internally. By the time I voice something, I've already weighed all of the options, considered every worst-case scenario possible, and am set in my decision. I don't need to discuss every angle over and over after this point. When I say, "I think I'll get a pedicure today," I don't need him to give me five reasons that I shouldn't. Yet, his extroverted self needs to do just that.

I leave the conversation angry because he has forbidden me to get my pedicure, when in fact he was just processing verbally. I've had my feelings hurt many times over the years, when Bob is left wondering what happened. Our personality differences will be more and more apparent as our story unfolds.

Neither Bob nor I were ready for our date to end after the movie. We decided to go to his parent's house and, you guessed it, watch another movie.

This time I left the decision of what movie to watch totally up to Bob. For two excruciating hours, I endured the ridiculousness of *Police Academy*. I tried to laugh with him; I may have fooled him at the time, but eventually, months, or probably years, later, I fessed up.

As painful as that movie watching experience was, I had a great time with Bob. He made me feel so comfortable. No one had ever been able to do that before. He genuinely wanted to know me, and somehow I'd allowed it.

Bob and I were engaged a few months later and married on December 13, 1986. Our family and friends must have thought we were crazy for getting married so quickly. This would be the first time of many that we did something most would view as foolish. If I thought our lives would be normal, I was in for a great shock.

Our wedding was simple, yet beautiful. We had unique music, few flowers, and a no-frills reception. I didn't want Bob to see me before the wedding, so we decided to do as many pictures separately before the ceremony as possible. I got ready in a classroom, while Bob got dressed in the church rectory.

Let me point out that this was no ordinary rectory. Formally the governor's mansion, this building is one of the most beautiful homes I have ever seen. It has a grand staircase with intricate woodwork and hand painted wallpaper. This home had three floors, two staircases, and at least three bedrooms and four bathrooms. Any bride would feel like a princess walking down the magnificent staircase in her white gown. But this princess would not get to walk down a grand staircase with her dress trailing behind her. This princess got dressed in a second-grade classroom.

If that wasn't enough, the photographer decided to take pictures of Bob and his groomsmen before my bridesmaids and me. This was back in the day when all cameras had film, and we were limited on the amount of shots. I was ready at 11:00 am, just as I was supposed to be, and waiting for the photographer to send for me. I was afraid to sit in the tiny desks in my gown, so I just stood leaning against the wall. The ceremony was to begin at 1:00, and when 11:55 rolled around, I was still standing in the classroom waiting. I started to get nervous. By the time I was sent for, it was after noon and we had to rush through the photo session.

When we got our proofs, I couldn't help but notice that over a third of the photos were of Bob without me. Bob by himself. Bob with his groomsmen helping him get ready. Bob with the bridesmaids. Extrovert, fun to be around Bob had the photographer laughing, and he lost track of how many photos he took, while my introvert self hid in the classroom.

I'm not bitter though. Not a bit.

The next day, we packed up my few belongings and we headed to our new life in Colorado Springs, Colorado. We decided not to go home to Kansas for Christmas that year. We talked to our parents on the phone, and then I cried. All day. Bob was flabbergasted. He couldn't understand why I wasn't happy on Christmas. "I am happy," I blubbered. "I just miss my family." This was the first time in our marriage that he was clueless on why I was upset and how to make me feel better. It wouldn't be the last. For the next decade at least, we were always in Topeka for Christmas.

Today's No; Tomorrow's Yes

From Lisa

December 24, 1992

B ob and I, along with our three-year-old daughter, Kelsey, stopped by the mall to pick up a few last minute items before heading to Topeka, Kansas, for Christmas. After finishing our shopping, we made the mistake of taking the escalator in the middle of the lobby.

We were halfway down when it happened. The Disney Store called to me. We love everything Disney and find it difficult to resist any opportunity to step into that magical world, even if it's just for a few minutes. I knew that we were in a hurry, but it was the Disney Store after all. I looked at Bob to find his eyes sparkling with excitement like I'm sure mine were. Glancing at Kelsey, I said, "I don't think we can risk it."

At the time, Kelsey was our only child, and we rarely made it out of any store without buying her something. I don't think we had ever left the Disney Store empty handed.

"Aw, come on. It'll be fine," Bob said.

I didn't actually believe him, but I wanted to look inside paradise just as much as he did. Before entering the store, I gave Kelsey the warning that since it was Christmas Eve, and she would be getting presents the next day, we would not be buying her anything in the store.

She agreed not to ask for anything. While all three of us perused and admired the wonderful things, Kelsey spotted something she could not live without—a Little Mermaid doll for the bathtub.

She gave me her cutest, most irresistible smile and said, "Isn't she beautiful Mommy?"

"Yes, she is. Maybe we can get her for you some other time."

"But Mom, what if she isn't here the next time?"

The fact is, Bob and I really wanted to get her the toy. There is nothing that brought us more joy than to make our precious daughter happy. And nothing made Kelsey happier than a Disney princess. However, I knew all she would be getting for Christmas the next day, and this little ten-dollar Ariel doll would be forgotten.

"We talked about this before we entered the store. The answer is no."

Then it began: the begging, reasoning, asking Daddy, and then, the fit.

Kelsey had become an expert at the fit. She did not disappoint us that day. I picked up my screaming child and rapidly left the store.

The fit continued. Determined to make it to the car as quickly as possible, I headed toward Dillard's. Oh, how I wished we hadn't parked outside that store.

Have you ever taken a hollering, flailing, small child into a Dillard's? It's not like Walmart, where in a situation like this one, the other mothers are smiling at you as if to say, "I've been there." Or maybe they're saying, "Better you than me." Either way, it is somewhat reassuring.

This was not the case in Dillard's. I rapidly marched through the store taking the most direct route possible to the much-needed exit. I could feel the stares of disapproval—could hear the tsk tsk, of people as they considered this out-of-control child. Not a pleasant experience, believe me. When we got to the door, I put Kelsey down to put her coat on.

She was not interested in leaving or wearing the coat, so she ran. Remember, this was Christmas Eve, and the store was packed with shoppers.

From my perspective, it looked as if people were moving out of Kelsey's way and then purposely putting themselves between us. After I weaved and dodged and said, "Excuse me" a thousand times, I tackled the little angel.

There is nothing Kelsey desired more at that moment than the Little Mermaid doll. That is all she could see. She couldn't begin to imagine what waited for her the next day.

I've been there.

1986

As I said before, when Bob and I got married, I couldn't wait to start a family. I wanted twelve children; Bob thought six would be enough. I figured the exact amount could be determined later. I was just anxious to get started.

To my disappointment, each month that first year proved to be devastating. We consulted doctors and had tests and finally, the results.

Infertile.

Has there ever been a word as hopeless as that? Imagine the driest desert where for miles there is no sign of life. No water. No shade. No relief. No hope.

My heart was that desert.

What was the purpose of my life if I couldn't have children? Why did God give me such a strong desire for children if he was going to deny me? He was God after all. He created the universe. He could easily help me get pregnant, despite what the doctors had said. But he chose not to.

Bob and I handled the devastating news differently. He threw himself into his work. I threw myself into being angry. I was furious with God. Why was he punishing me?

We were open to adoption. I even let myself get excited about it. But, as we researched various adoption agencies, we hit roadblock after roadblock.

We didn't make enough money for this one; we weren't married long enough for that one. And with every disappointment, my fury with God grew.

Bitterness encompassed me. Bob mostly tried to avoid the subject. But one day he said, "Someday, Lisa, we'll be able to look back at this time and see why this is happening to us."

I said, "No matter what, I will never, ever understand why God is doing this to me."

Life went on and we finally decided to get on a waiting list for the Catholic Charities Adoption agency in Colorado Springs. The wait was supposed to be four to six years, so by the time our names would come up to the top of the list, we would have been married the required three years.

In the spring of 1989 we received a call from Catholic Charities. They had a birthmother who was due within the next couple months who was carrying a bi-racial baby. They wanted to be able to give her a choice between the only couples on the waiting list that would be open to such a child—Bob and me and one other couple.

I let myself hope. I bought baby things and started putting the baby's room together. To our disappointment, the birthmother chose the other couple.

A few weeks later, my mom called to tell me about a trip she had taken with her sisters to the Shrine of the Infant Jesus of Prague in Prague, Oklahoma. Thousands of people had claimed to have their prayers answered after visiting the Shrine. She had put in a prayer request for God to bring us a baby. I appreciated it, but had little faith that anything would happen. I had said thousands of prayers and still had no baby.

From Bob

Recently I presented a mega-workshop at the National Catholic Youth Conference (NCYC) in Indianapolis, Indiana. After my session, a couple approached me. Before we ever began speaking, I noticed that the wife was tearing up. I knew exactly what they were going to talk about. She seemed to be struggling to hold back the tears, so her husband started the conversation. He said, "Thank you for talking about the adoption of your daughter. We have been suffering with infertility since we got married." Actually I thought suffering was the perfect word because it felt like every month a lot of suffering went on. It's hard to see the person you love upset month after month after month after month because she began her cycle, and any hope and dream of a child for that month was dashed. As I spoke to this couple, I was reminded of how real and painful this suffering with infertility was for Lisa and me.

At the time we were going through this, we were living 533 miles from our family and friends. This made everything far more difficult for Lisa. I had a natural outlet for friendships through the church that I worked for, but Lisa did not. As I said before, I spent my entire childhood making new friendships, so finding friends for me was still easy. Lisa had grown up in the same house, going to the same school with the same friends year after year. Making friends did not come easily for her. It was hard to understand that at first. It was very frustrating that she would complain about not having friends but absolutely hated going out and doing things with other people. Grant it, by other people, I meant my youth ministry team. During that time, Lisa retreated into herself. I on the other hand avoided my pain by pouring myself into work. I kept myself busy and my mind occupied with building a youth ministry program. One thing I've learned over my thirty-plus years in ministry is that very rarely will a priest discourage you from working. I put all of my energy into my job and building relationships with both the youth and my youth ministry team. It was easy to justify because I was doing a good thing. I was helping kids grow closer to Christ, while my wife was at home infuriated with him. Now, I don't want to make it sound like I was a total jerk. I did talk with Lisa about our infertility on a regular basis. Every month it was unavoidable.

I dealt with it like all control freaks would deal with it. I wanted to fix it and make it better. I mistakenly thought that I could fill that hole for Lisa—that somehow I could fix it. The reality is nothing I could have said or done could have taken away the pain. Being a major optimist, I always seem to find good, even in bad situations, which looking back now probably drove Lisa crazy. Instead of validating Lisa's feelings or dwelling on my own, I would try to say hopeful things like, "This is happening for a reason," or

"God has a plan for us." Instead of making it better, I made Lisa feel more isolated and alone. I couldn't understand Lisa's pessimism any more than I could comprehend advanced algebraic equations. Just when my optimism eased the discomfort of infertility, Lisa's pessimism brought me crashing down to reality. Her reality.

Even today my optimistic side looks back on those days, and I see the silver lining. I think we were better parents because of that time of extended longing for children. It forced us to cling on to one another and grow in our relationship. When you say in your wedding vows for better or worse, there isn't much that I can imagine worse than dealing with infertility. It felt a lot like drowning. The difference between Lisa and me is that I reached for a life preserver while she let herself be pulled under. Somehow I managed to keep ahold of her long enough for her to experience her miracle.

~~Forgotten~~ Remembered

From Bob

Summer 1992

"Come on Kelsey, you can jump." Lisa urged. "I promise, I'll catch you."

I watched from the window as Lisa tried to encourage Kelsey into the pool in my in-law's back yard. My daughter loved the water. However, she didn't love getting her face wet. Something about submerging her head in the pool terrified her.

Next to the four-foot above ground pool stood a small deck. The deck was old and, let's just say, a little rickety. But for some reason, Kelsey preferred the safety of the unsteady deck to the possibility that Lisa would not catch her.

"I'm scared, Mommy."

"It's okay Sweetie, Trust me."

Kelsey backed to the edge of the deck and said, "Okay, one, two, three!" She ran toward the pool. I smiled, sure she would finally have the courage to actually jump. When Kelsey reached the edge, she skidded to a stop, threw her arms in the air, and while backing away hollered, "No, no, no, no, no."

Lisa laughed, finding our daughter's reaction adorable. Again she begged, "Come on Kelsey, I promise I'll catch you."

"Okay, one, two, three!" She ran forward only to stop at the edge and back away screaming, "No, no, no."

This went on several more times. Lisa was very patient, but I could tell that the "cuteness" of the situation was wearing off.

Finally, we received a little help from the old deck. Just as Kelsey tried to stop at the edge, one of the boards bent just enough to propel her into the pool.

Although shocked by this, Lisa managed to catch her, but not before Kelsey's head went all the way under. To our surprise, Kelsey emerged from the water laughing and yelling, "Again!"

Whoever the genius was that said small children have short attention spans obviously was not familiar with kids of this age. We couldn't wait for Kelsey to jump in, and now we found ourselves wishing she would want to stop.

We do that with God. We say, "God, I trust you. I'll make you the center of my life." And then something happens and we back away hollering, "No, no, no."

The next day we say, "Okay, now I'm really ready to trust you, God." And before we know it we are running again yelling, "No, no, no."

Sometimes life makes no sense. Sometimes we find ourselves in situations we can't understand. Trust sounds good in theory, but when it comes right down to it, instead of leaping in knowing God will catch us, we turn away.

When Lisa and I found ourselves struggling to start a family, trust was difficult. Sometimes it seemed impossible. We wanted kids desperately and couldn't understand God's reasons for denying us.

The adoption process seemed endless. All the hoops we had to jump through frustrated us. The seemingly interminable waiting and the intrusion of social workers who peruse through your past and present, trying to determine if we were "fit parents" all seemed unfair. So many unpleasant things we endured that people who have children naturally never have to face.

It's amazing how slow time moves when you really want something. While you wait, you feel like you're trying to climb out of a pit of which you cannot see the top. You can't imagine what it will be like when and if you finally reach it.

In the spring of 1989, I was offered a job in Leawood, Kansas, as a parish youth minister. I liked my job and parish in Colorado Springs, so I turned him down. When I told Lisa about it, she was very upset.

For a long time, my wife had wanted to move closer to home. The ten-hour drive was just too far for her. Because I worked long hours, she was alone much of the time. As devastating as our infertility was for me, for her it was unbearable. Basically, she needed her mother.

My father-in-law told me before Lisa and I were married that in marriage, you can either be right or happy. Choose one. That day I chose happiness, and in June, we were on our way to our new life.

A few months later, a parishioner, who was also a doctor, approached me after Mass. "I have a doctor friend in Missouri who has a patient that has decided to place her baby for adoption. She really wants her baby to be raised Catholic. I just came from adoration, and for some reason, I feel I should ask if you would be interested in adopting her baby"

It took every bit of self-control not to jump up and down and scream. I calmly informed him that in fact my wife and I had wanted to adopt.

Lisa and I were ecstatic. We let ourselves hope again, only this time, we also held on to fear. Fear that this would be another false alarm. Fear that something would happen that would prevent us from being parents. Again.

Five weeks later, we picked up our daughter, Kelsey Renee Perron, from the hospital where she was born. We placed her in her car seat in the back of our tiny Ford Festiva. Lisa insisted on sitting in back with her. As we drove away, I couldn't help but keep looking in the rear view mirror. Part of me feared that someone would be running behind our car screaming, "Wait. There's been a terrible mistake."

Lisa stared at our new daughter in disbelief. Was this really happening? She managed to tear her eyes away long enough to open a packet our lawyer had handed to us earlier that day informing us that its contents were from Kelsey's birth family.

There were clothes, some family heirlooms, and two envelopes—one from Kelsey's birthmother and one from her birth-grandmother. Lisa decided to read the letter from the grandmother first. The first sentence read, "Last spring, I took a pilgrimage to the Shrine of the Infant Jesus of

Prague in Oklahoma to put in a prayer request for the best outcome for both mother and baby." Kelsey's birth-grandmother was there around the same time Lisa's mom had been. And God had answered both prayers.

Lisa had been feeling punished and abandoned by God. She had been running away hollering, "No, no, no." And yet, she held the proof in her hands that in fact, she had been wrong.

God had moved us from Colorado to the very parish we needed to in order to meet the doctor who first brought us news of Kelsey. Kelsey's birthmother relocated as well to stay with her aunt in Missouri, where she would become the patient of the doctor friend.

No words can describe the enormity of that miracle.

Yesterday's no had made today's yes possible. Like Kelsey at the Disney Store, Lisa focused on the no. She was so busy running and screaming and throwing a metaphorical fit, she couldn't stop and consider that tomorrow's yes would prove to be far greater than anything she could have imagined.

If I would've had things my way, we would have had at least two children up to this point. But neither one of them would have been Kelsey, and that thought is incomprehensible.

God had a plan for Lisa and me. That plan involved a "no" that broke our hearts. The death of a dream is more painful than it sounds—some dreams more than others.

From Lisa

I need to back up a bit. I want to get real about what those childless years were like for me. I already told you how angry I was. Being angry with God is not the kind of thing that I could talk about. My husband worked for the Catholic Church; it wasn't appropriate for me to voice my negative feelings towards God. Bob wasn't comfortable with them either.

Mostly, we avoided the subject of our infertility. However, once a month, it was impossible, especially in the months that I was a day or two late getting my period. Those months I would almost let myself hope. I would think to myself, always to myself, that God had given me my miracle. But then my period would come, and I would dissolve into a puddle of despair.

Because of my bicornuate uterus, I suffered from endometriosis and cystic ovaries that caused extreme pain every month. I would often be doubled over in both physical and emotional pain. The pain was just another reminder that my womb remained empty along with my arms.

Every pregnancy announcement by friends and family only increased my fury. Why God? Why them and not me? I was always thrilled to welcome nieces and nephews and babies of friends when they arrived, but every second of witnessing other women experience what I so desperately wanted filled me with envy. And, if one of those women complained about how the pregnancy caused her discomfort, I wanted to shake her. She had no idea how lucky she was. I would've given anything to be able to experience morning sickness, an aching back, or constant indigestion. But God had said no.

I felt totally abandoned. Forgotten. Like an outsider, just like I did when I was that little fourth-grader sitting on the tile floor of the family counselor's office.

The truth is, I've never been very memorable. I met one of our friends from Steubenville for the first time on at least four different occasions. This used to bother me immensely, but I've come to accept it as a side effect of being introverted.

I have misunderstood this part of my personality for most of my life. I just attributed people's lack of remembering me to my utter un-specialness. If I were more remarkable, I would be worth recalling.

In the summer of 1989, Bob and I decided to visit my grandfather in Nebraska. This would be the first time I would visit my Nebraskan relatives without any other member of my immediate family, and I was scared to death. I didn't voice it at the time, but this visit was kind of a test—a test to see if I was worth Granddad remembering me. I internally coached myself to be like my sister, whom no one ever seemed to forget. I would go into his house and act like her. When my step-grandmother, Dorothy, opened the door for me, I marched across the room and threw my arms around his neck. He hugged me back but when he finished he said, "And, what was your name?"

My heart sank. I had failed. My own grandfather didn't even know my name. Dorothy spoke up, "Clair, this is Lisa. I told you she was coming."

He smiled, "Oh. That's right. Lisa."

"Please excuse him," Dorothy said. "He has a hard time remembering these days."

Luckily, Bob is never at a loss for words and he carried the conversation for the rest of the day. I couldn't speak from the huge lump living in my throat.

Memory is such a curious thing. Several times while we played cards during that visit, he'd ask, "What game are we playing?"

"Pitch, Clair." Dorothy would remind him.

Somehow he couldn't remember what he did the day before, but he recalled every detail about the dust storm in 1936. Right before we left him for the last time, he said,

"Lisa." Relief flooded me. He remembered. Then he said, " Carv has a daughter named Lisa."

Sigh.

"I know, Granddad. That's me." He looked at me with a confused look. He couldn't reconcile the woman in front of him with the little girl he remembered. I hugged him and told him I loved him and left. My mind knew that he was suffering from dementia, and that was why he didn't know me. But my heart was harder to convince.

Granddad died three months later.

I've relived that visit many times in the years since my grandfather's death. Every time I had to be introduced to someone for the second, third, or even fourth time, I remembered the words of Granddad, "And, what was your name?" If I was so hard to recollect while I lived, how was I ever going to be remembered after I died? Had God forgotten me? Why was I even here?

~~Adoptive~~ Mother

From Lisa

When it first became apparent that in order to have a family, Bob and I would have to adopt, I had an unvoiced fear. Would I really feel like a mother if I hadn't given birth to my baby? I was truly afraid that being an adoptive mother was somehow secondary and that my motherhood wouldn't count. I held that fear all of the way into the hospital where we would pick up our first daughter.

On November 17, 1989, Bob and I traveled to Joplin, Missouri, to pick up our baby. We had already met with our lawyer in Kansas City, Kansas, and would meet with our Missouri lawyer in Joplin. Since we lived in a different state than the one Kelsey was born, we needed an Interstate Compact that would allow us to take our baby across the state line to our home in Olathe, Kansas. I don't think I'd taken a complete breath since Kelsey's birth. I was excited, stressed, worried, hopeful, and afraid something would go wrong.

It was obvious by the office décor that our lawyer loved the outdoors. The lobby had comfortable leather chairs: at least they looked comfortable. I was too nervous to sit down. After a few minutes, we were escorted into a conference room with dark wood paneling and a long table. Bob handed him the paperwork to be presented to the Missouri court, and, in turn, the lawyer handed us a large manila envelope containing items from Kelsey's birth family. "There's some letters, some clothes, pictures and, I don't know, some religious family heirlooms or something."

I held on to that envelope like it contained highly fragile china. I didn't open the envelope then. I was afraid that I would somehow jinx us. The lawyer was gone for about thirty minutes before he returned with the paperwork signed by the judge that gave us custody of our baby.

Our lawyer rode in the passenger seat of our tiny car on the way to the hospital. He said, "If this baby turns out anything like her birthmother, she will be someone truly special." I didn't doubt that a bit. I knew that she had kept Kelsey in her room the whole time she was in the hospital. This made some of our family worry that she would change her mind and decide to keep her baby. It gave me comfort. Our baby had known love from the very moment of her birth.

As we walked into the hospital, I imagined going to the nursery to see our baby like I'd seen in the movies. Instead, we were herded into a private room and left there. It seemed like our presence in the hospital was a huge secret. A few minutes later a nurse arrived pushing a bassinette carrying the most beautiful baby girl I'd ever seen.

I wanted to scoop her into my arms immediately. The nurse had other plans. Before we would be allowed to hold our baby, she wanted to go over the release paperwork. She started rattling off a list of tasks we needed to do for our baby's care. When she noticed that we couldn't take our eyes off our precious child, she snatched Kelsey out of the bassinette and held her so we couldn't see her. "I need you to pay attention to what I'm telling you." We said nothing. We were so afraid of causing something to happen that would deny us our baby.

When the nurse finished the list and extracted our signatures, she finally handed our baby to me. All of my fears about whether or not I would feel like a mother were forgotten. There was no doubt in my mind or my heart that I held *my* child in my arms. I handed her to Bob and marveled at what a natural father he was. About five minutes in, we decided it was time to leave—again out of fear of something falling through.

I dressed Kelsey in a pink cheerleader sleeper and put her in a Minnie Mouse bunting to keep her warm. The nurse told us that usually she has to push mothers to their cars in a wheelchair while the mothers held their baby. But since I didn't need a wheelchair, she would have to carry Kelsey to the car and make sure we had a proper car seat. In the elevator, the nurse looked at me and said, "So, you decided to do this the easy way, huh."

I looked her straight in the eyes and said, "There was nothing easy about this."

She ignored me the rest of the way to the car. Despite the chilly reception at the hospital, Bob and I were overjoyed to be bringing our baby home. I sat in the back seat with Kelsey and opened the precious envelope. It held a small photo album with little slips of paper with captions written by Kelsey's birthmother. There were two small envelopes: one contained a letter from Kelsey's birth-grandmother and one from her birthmother. As Bob has already told you, I read the one from Kelsey's grandmother first. I cried all the way through it. I cried because I realized that when I felt forgotten by God and fussed at him for not giving me a baby, he was working without my knowledge to make it happen. I cried because the words Kelsey's grandmother wrote were so full of hope and love for our little girl. And I cried because another mother was mourning after having to say goodbye to this precious baby.

The letter from her birthmother was shorter; I'm sure every word cost her dearly. Along with the letter was a beautiful poem she had written for Kelsey. My heart ached for her even in the midst of my joy.

The manila envelope also contained a cute little yellow outfit that one day my granddaughter would wear on her way home from the hospital. There was also some holy water in a Blessed Mary shaped bottle from Our Lady of Lourdes in France. I was right to take such care with that envelope.

On the second night we were home with Kelsey, as I rocked her in the middle of the night, my heart overflowed with love for my daughter, and I felt a special connection to her birthmother. Years later, I penned this poem about the moment.

Three Hearts

As I rock you in the middle of the night,
You melt into my chest as only newborns can.
Heat burns within my heart.
Could I ever love anyone more?

My heart longs for all of the moments

Of your life that I have missed.
I yearn to feel you grow in me,
Your heart beating with mine.

Yet if I would have been the one
To carry you before your birth,
You wouldn't have the same graceful fingers
Or the spot on your forehead I love so much.

Or the long dark eyelashes
That bring out the blue in your eyes.
You wouldn't be you;
And that thought, I cannot bear.

I think of the woman
Who gave you life.
Two nights ago it was she
Who rocked you in the night

Memorizing your features
Etching them in her mind.
She longed to hold on forever
But that was not to be.

Your first mother was very young
Too young, she knew,
To be able to give you all that you deserve

No matter how much she longed to.

I feel the yearning of her heart
For all the moments she will miss,
Your first smile, your wedding day,
Or the day when you too have a daughter.

Her touch still lingers
From the last time she held you.
Her last kiss's imprint is still on your brow.
In that moment, my heart beats with hers.

How heavy her empty arms must be.
How hollow she must feel.
How strong she was to let you go.
Could she ever love anyone more?

I hear your sleep-filled breathing
And relish your newborn scent.
Somehow I pull you closer.
Your heart beats with mine.

How will I ever convey to you
How much that you are loved.
First by her and then by me,
Could we ever love anyone more?

OUR ~~ADOPTIVE~~ FAMILY

From Bob

1997

K elsey chewed her fingernails, drew her courage and blurted out, "Dad, can I have a bra?"

My first inclination was to laugh. After all, my daughter was only in the third grade. My second reaction was one of panic. My daughter was already in the third grade, and all too soon she would actually need a bra. Where was all the time going?

Not knowing the correct way to answer this question, I said what all good fathers say. "Let's ask your mother."

When we arrived home, Kelsey carried her books up to her room, which gave me the perfect opportunity to consult with Lisa in the kitchen.

"You're not going to believe this, but on the way home Kelsey asked if she could have a bra."

I waited for the expected reaction—laughter. Instead my wife said, "That's so awesome that she trusts you enough to ask you for something like that."

Taken aback, I tried in vain to understand what I'd just heard. I expected answers and had none. I asked for clarification. "What should I tell her?"

Lisa answered with a wide grin. "You'll think of something."

How could she throw responsibility for this back to me? She was Kelsey's mother after all. Wasn't it her job to take care of things like feminine undergarments? Having nothing more to say on the matter, I returned to work.

Kelsey's question haunted me for the rest of the day and half the night. By the time I was ready to wake her up the next morning, I came up with the perfect way to handle the situation.

I tiptoed into her room, sat on the edge of her bed and gently rubbed her back. (She loved it when I did that.) "Kelsey honey, it's time to wake up."

"I don't want to get up. It's too early." I had to admit, I agreed with her on that point. It was still dark after all.

"I know, but you got to get up and get ready for school. And after school, I'm going to take you to Walmart."

Her face lit up; her sleepiness vanished. "Why are we going to Walmart?"

"Well, I'm going to buy you a gas can."

"What?"

"A gas can. So in case you run out of gas, you can put gas in your car."

Her precious little forehead crunched up in confusion. "But, I don't even have a car."

This was it, the teaching moment I had been waiting for. "Well honey, that's kind of how I see you wanting the bra."

Kelsey was a very bright young lady, so she caught on to my meaning rather quickly. She hopped out of bed and ran down the steps to tattle on me.

In the mean time, I continued with my morning rituals. By the time I got out of the shower, order was restored to the house, and I drove Kelsey to school. The bra was not mentioned on the way, so I thought the matter was handled. I should have known better.

Kelsey didn't talk much on the way home either. She must have still been upset with me. To my surprise, however, she bounced into the house, delivered a letter to my wife, and disappeared up the stairs.

I looked over Lisa's shoulder to find an eloquently written letter explaining why she needed a bra. Evidently, her best friend had one, and when the other girls in her class discovered it (she showed it to them), two of her other friends arrived at school the next day wearing bras identical to hers.

I still didn't understand why an eight-year-old needed a bra, but my wife was moved.

I went to Walmart.

That story was a reminder to me that sometimes we think we know what is going to bring us happiness. We get so caught up in the immediate longing without realizing that it's just not the right time. Kelsey was sure that having a bra like her friends would make her happy. And as we get older it only gets worse. We think, "If only I had the right job, the right family, the right car, or the right house, I could be happy." I knew that Kelsey's bra was not the key to her happiness just as God knows that many times I pursue perceived wants/needs in vain. I am so grateful that we have a very patient and merciful God who sometimes has plans that are better than we can imagine; we just have to wait.

From Lisa

Through the years, there have been so many times when I almost forgot that Kelsey was adopted. More than once, I've started filling out the family medical history section in the paperwork at the doctor's office and realize that I don't know the answers to the questions. Kelsey fit into our family so naturally that it seemed that she had always been ours. She came to us so young that I didn't dream that she would ever have issues with being adopted. I was very naïve.

In every way, I just wanted to live like our family was just like everyone else's. There was no doubt that I was Kelsey's mother. But sometimes thoughts would wriggle into my head that reminded me that I was not her first. I'll never forget the first time Kelsey told me that she wished she lived with her birthmother. I don't remember what prompted her outburst, but her words hit me hard. It not only felt like a rejection from her but also served as a reminder that there was another mother out there who could claim Kelsey's esteem—another mother with a biological connection with my daughter that I feared was stronger than the one I shared with her.

After a few sleepless nights, I realized that Kelsey hadn't meant her words as a rejection of me. Her saying she wished she lived with her birthmother was like when most other children say, "I wish I had different parents." I know I had said that as a child multiple times. I didn't mean it then any more than Kelsey meant it when she said it.

Not a day has gone by that I haven't thought about Kelsey's birthmother. I feel a bond to the woman borne out of mutual love of our child. Most of the time, I think only of the miracle of adoption and how it allowed me to become a mother. It's difficult not to dwell on the enormity of the gratitude I feel from the privilege. The problem with always focusing on the celebratory aspect of adoption is that it denies the tragedy every adoption begins with—a mother is separated from her child, and a child is separated from his or her mother.

Like I said, in the beginning, I thought that since Kelsey came to us at three days old, she would not be affected much by being adopted. I was the only mother she knew, and surely that would be enough. My husband and I spoke openly about her adoption because we knew Kelsey had the right to know about her origins. It never occurred to me that she would feel loss over not knowing her biological mother. I now know that it doesn't matter what age an adopted child finds their forever family, there is still a part of them that longs for the unknown. There is nothing Bob or I can say or do that will fill the hole that was left by Kelsey's birthmother. The best we can do is acknowledge her feelings and do whatever we can to help her discover the answers she needs.

I knew then as I know now that Kelsey was meant to be ours even before Bob and I ever learned about her. For some reason, God meant for Kelsey to touch her birthmother's life before she touched ours, and we are so very grateful.

~~ANOTHER NEGATIVE~~
POSITIVE PREGNANCY TEST

From Lisa

It was a Saturday morning in November of 1994. I had been preparing all week for Kelsey's fifth birthday party. We had purchased a battery operated ride-on jeep for her birthday and couldn't wait to see our daughter drive it. The cake was made, the decorations put up, and the food was almost ready. Everything looked perfect, but something felt different.

I had been trying to ignore the fact that my period was a few days late. I normally wasn't late and when I was, I was rarely this late. I decided to take a home pregnancy test just so I could let go of the possibility of a miracle pregnancy. An hour before the guests were supposed to arrive I locked myself in the bathroom. As I waited for the results, I hoped that one hour would be long enough for me to get my crying over with and all evidence of devastation wiped from my face before our families arrived.

It was positive.

I stared at that little stick, checked the box to make sure I was reading it correctly, showed it to Bob, and stared some more. I couldn't believe it. I wouldn't believe it until I was told by a doctor that I was, in fact, pregnant.

Kelsey's birthday party was great fun. She loved her jeep and the time playing with all of her cousins. Bob and I loved every minute of it, but in the back of our minds we wondered if there was going to be more to celebrate.

Two days later, we got the news. I was pregnant. I should've been screaming, crying, jumping, and dancing for joy. Instead, I was numb. I was paralyzed with fear that at any moment, my miracle would be taken away. Bob wanted to call our families immediately. I couldn't just yet.

"I thought you'd be more excited than this," Bob said, bewildered at my mellow reaction.

"I am excited," I said, "just..." I didn't have words for my feelings—for my fear. I felt exactly like I did on my way into the hospital to pick up Kelsey. Excited, yet reluctant. If I didn't acknowledge the full extent of my joy over my pregnancy, my disappointment when it failed would be lessened.

Bob wore me down, and I allowed him to call our parents before the day ended. "I'll bet you're overjoyed," they said. And I was. I just couldn't show it yet.

When I was eight weeks along, I started spotting. It wasn't a lot of blood, but enough to bring that I told you so monster roaring to the surface. I had an ultrasound, and although it was too early to really make out the baby, we could see the tiny heartbeat, which was a great sign. The doctor said that it would be rare to miscarry after seeing such a strong heartbeat but not unheard of. He told us one in four pregnancies end in miscarriage, a statistic that I'd not known. He sent me home to rest, which to me meant something else. I sat around all weekend just waiting for a miscarriage to start. Thankfully it didn't.

The next few weeks went by and just when I started to feel confident in a successful pregnancy, I started spotting again. We went through the same routine, ultrasound, seeing the heartbeat, and sent home to wait. This happened once more after this, and each time we were sent on the roller coaster ride of potential lost hope.

I held everything about this pregnancy at a distance. I wouldn't allow myself to fully enjoy all of the wonderful things happening inside me because I was sure that as soon as I embraced the experience, it would be snatched from me. As I look back, I see how little faith I had in God's goodness. I never doubted his power to produce miracles, only his willingness to do so.

From Bob

To say that I was excited at the news of Lisa's pregnancy would be a total understatement. I wanted to tell everyone I knew immediately, and I did. As Lisa's pregnancy progressed, I began getting a little concerned about how Kelsey would react to no longer being the only child—the most amazing child in her parent's universe. I wanted her to feel included in the process. So, when the day arrived that Lisa was to have her twenty-week ultrasound, I thought it would be a great idea to bring our five-year-old along. Unfortunately, I had made the mistake of telling Kelsey that we were going to see a picture of the baby.

Now they have 4D ultrasounds where the images you see on screen can be almost like actual photos. At the very least, it is easy for the untrained eye to see that it is a human infant that they are seeing. Back then, ultrasound images were not nearly as clear. They were just fuzzy one-dimensional images. It was more like looking at white blobs in the midst of a black hole. I at least, found the blinking white dot of the baby's heartbeat exciting. Kelsey was not as easily impressed.

The nurse caught on to Kelsey's frustration and started telling us what she saw on the screen.

"Here's the little legs and feet, and here's the arms. You can see the eyes and nose here."

Kelsey and I were like, "If you say so."

The nurse took the little pointer and made a circular movement around what even I could tell was the baby's head. She said, "Here you can see the baby's brain."

Kelsey lost her mind. She began jumping and skipping and saying in a sing-song voice, "The baby has a brain, the baby has a brain."

When I questioned her about her reaction, she told me, "Dad the baby has a brain! It is a girl!"

Thankfully, she was right.

ANOTHER DAUGHTER

From Lisa

Mackenzie Rose Perron arrived via C-section on July 15, 1995. Although only a week early, she was tiny. I had been telling the doctor for a few weeks that I didn't think that she had been growing. Despite my belly measuring smaller each week, he said that I appeared smaller because my baby had dropped, so they couldn't get an accurate measurement of my uterus. A different doctor performed my surgery and he told us that it was obvious that our five-pound four-ounce baby hadn't grown for weeks. Part of our infertility issues was that I have a bicornate uterus. Instead of my uterus being shaped like an upside down triangle, mine was more of a heart shape. Mackenzie had been crammed on one side of the heart so she had no more room to grow. This was also the cause of her being breech, requiring the emergency C-section.

But she was here, our miracle.

One of the qualities that I enjoyed most about Mackenzie was her huge imagination. While Kelsey required more direct attention from us, Mackenzie entertained herself often. It was impossible to punish her by putting her in timeout. You could put her in a corner facing a white wall and she would be able to pass the time joyfully using her two hands as puppets.

One day Bob asked her what she was doing when it appeared her two hands were talking to each other. She said that one hand was Big Head, who was just a talking head on a wall. The other hand was Princess Laura. Somewhere I have a book that I helped her write about the adventure she acted out in her head. She illustrated the book and I wrote down the story.

Mackenzie had an imaginary friend called Ghost Ghost, who went with her wherever she went. We'd have to pull up an extra chair for Ghost Ghost when we went to restaurants. We never had to order him food, however, because Mackenzie was always willing to share hers.

Speaking of ghosts, we had a ritual every night when we tucked Mackenzie into bed. She couldn't go to sleep until all of the ghosts were thrown out of her room. Bob and I would run around the room jumping to catch the ghosts that Mackenzie pointed out to us and we would get rid of them. One night Bob was just about to throw a ghost out that he had just caught when Mackenzie said, "Not that one, Dad! That one's yellow. The yellow ones can stay. Remember?"

From Bob

I loved being Kelsey's dad, and I was getting pretty good at it. I couldn't imagine being able to love a human any more. It was an utter surprise that when I saw Mackenzie for the first time, my heart somehow expanded enough to love both of them completely. Each of them beautiful and unique in their own way, and I felt so lucky that I got to be their dad. I have so many precious memories of these two when they were young.

One of my favorite memories of Mackenzie involved church. Mackenzie loved church. She knew every word that Father Pat spoke during Mass, and on most Sundays, she said them right along with him. She could've easily filled in if necessary.

On one particular Sunday, Mackenzie stood in the doorway with her hands on her hips gazing at the church as if to say, "Let the games begin."

As Lisa has already told you, Mackenzie had an incredible imagination. That came in handy while entertaining her three-year-old self at church. To us, the little cushion that we kneel on is called a kneeler. To Mackenzie, it was her pony. She would bounce up and down on them saying, "Yee haw!" Lisa and I spent almost the entire Mass reminding her to be quiet, but as we all know, there is no such thing as whispering when you are three.

That day after communion, I decided to try and distract her from her pony and use this opportunity as a teaching moment. "Look up there Mackenzie," I said while pointing to the cups on the altar. "That's Jesus. And see now Father Pat is going to put Jesus in the tabernacle."

"What's a tabernacle?"

"See that beautiful, gold box up there, that's the tabernacle. And Father is going to put Jesus in it."

Horrified, she asked, "He's going to put Jesus in a box?"

"It's okay," I reassured her. "Jesus likes it in that box."

There's a moment just after communion, when the music is over and Father sits silently in his chair on the altar. It's a prayerful moment. On this Sunday, the church was completely silent. I sat there smiling at Lisa, proud of myself for instructing my daughter about the tabernacle. I was such a great dad.

Then all of the sudden, Mackenzie jumped to her feet and hollered, "Don't worry Jesus! I'll get you out of there!"

Everyone laughed. Except me. At first, because of my embarrassment, I was angry. I didn't know what to do. I tried to think of some punishment I could give my daughter to teach her not to yell in church.

But then it dawned on me that Mackenzie wasn't trying to misbehave. Jesus was her friend, and she wanted nothing else but to rescue her friend from the box.

She didn't learn that from some theology book or great homily. She just knew.

OUR FIRST SON

From Lisa

My second pregnancy was much different than my first. Instead of keeping my pregnancy at a distance like before, I relished every experience. I greeted every bit of nausea or indigestion enthusiastically because I was just so incredibly grateful for the chance to experience the miracle of birth all over again. I loved being pregnant. There is no experience that can match the miracle of feeling your baby move and grow inside your own body.

Robert Carvel Perron arrived a month early, also via C section, on May 26, 1999, weighing six pounds and eleven ounces. From day one, this boy has had my heart. He is sweet, laid back, empathetic, and at times short-tempered. (I have no idea where he gets that from.) Both of my homemade babies were easy. I don't think that it was because they were born from me, but that God knew whom he would be sending to us next.

In the summer of 2000, we decided to move to Denison, Iowa. What brought us to Denison is a story for another day. Denison is a quaint town of about 8300 people. It was the birthplace of Donna Reed, who starred in the movie *It's a Wonderful Life*. Needless to say, they took Christmas very seriously there.

I loved it in Denison. The community welcomed us warmly, and we made some lifelong friends there. We met a young couple who had an adorable four-year-old daughter that they had adopted from Korea. God had placed the desire to adopt internationally in my heart years before, so I loved spending time with this nice family. Cathy and Dennis introduced us to the Holt International Adoption Agency, which we would go through a couple years later when we adopted Isaiah.

We lived in a cute two-story house with a screened-in porch and a walkout basement. It is there that I first started homeschooling my oldest two girls. As much as I loved that house and that town, after only nine months, God called us to move to a camp/retreat center about forty-five minutes west of Des Moines, where Bob served as the Executive Director of the St. Thomas More Center and the diocesan youth Director for the diocese of Des Moines.

Housing was provided for us, which at first was a huge adjustment for me. We moved from my cute house on a

quiet street in a sweet little town to a tiny A-frame house
that hadn't been remodeled in decades. (It had carpet in the
kitchen and bathroom, and the edge of the laminate
countertop had been nailed into place!) Every afternoon,
Japanese beetles somehow made their way into our house
and when you vacuumed them up, they smelled like dirty
feet. I cried when I saw this house for the first time and
many times after that. Being outsiders in a close-knit camp
community wasn't conducive to a warm welcome.
Thankfully, however they did change out the flooring in the
kitchen and bathroom and replaced the countertop shortly
after we moved in. Eventually, they built a bigger house for
our family.

We moved in to the A-frame a few weeks before
summer camp was to start. We barely got settled in when
the fun began. The kids loved growing up at that camp and
we loved watching them interact with the campers and
staff. Bobby was particularly interested in the man who
took care of the property and provided trail rides on
horseback for the campers. Bobby has always been a great
observer and for some reason, he found Duane fascinating.
Bobby had a little battery operated ride-on tractor that he
used to ride with both of his legs on the same side because
that's how Duane often rode his four-wheeler. He insisted
on getting cowboy boots and a cowboy hat so he could
dress like Duane, and when we went to Disney World, he
picked a Grumpy hat and beard as his souvenir and called it

his Duane hat. (Duane had white hair and a white beard.) One day when we were out at the horse barn, Bobby pointed behind the barn and told me that it was Duane's bathroom. I didn't question him about that further.

When Bobby was nine he said he wanted to to run for president. So, Mackenzie helped him create a commercial for his campaign. Along with Bobby's best friend Sam, they came up with a minute and a half long video. The introduction read, "Are you looking for someone who is against murder, littering, and poopy girls on the playground? Then Bobby Perron is the candidate for you." I think he may have been on to something.

From Bob

November 2005

M y boy. I had always dreamed having a son. Don't get me wrong, I love my daughters, and I wouldn't trade them for the world, but when Bobby was born, I felt complete somehow.

It is a minor miracle that my son's name is Robert (Bobby). I never thought I would be allowed to name a child because Lisa had this crazy idea that I wouldn't pick good names. I once told her that we should name our kids Erin, Darren, and Sharon Perron. After that day, she never took my name suggestions seriously. I always wanted to name a son Robert, but Lisa thought that there were far too many of us. I come from a long line of Roberts. My great-grandfather was a Robert. My grandfather was a Robert, my dad was a Robert, and my mom is Roberta. Do you see the pattern here? It was only due to horrible circumstances that my son was named Robert. My dad had suffered with ALS for seven years and passed away just six weeks before Bobby's birth. It was a really tough time for us, and Lisa's heart softened toward the name. Now, neither one of us can imagine him having any other name.

Bobby was a very laid back child. If you asked him 'what's up" he would respond by saying, "Good things, Dad, good things." He was such a gentle soul. One of my favorite memories of him growing up was while driving down the road one day, I looked at my son through the rearview mirror. "What do you want for Christmas, Bobby?"

He narrowed his eyes and thought for a moment. "I want a tuxedo."

That was unexpected. How many six-year-old boys would ask for a tuxedo for Christmas? "Why's that, son?"

Bobby grinned widely. "Because my mom's the greatest mom in the world, and I want to take her to dinner to tell her thank you. My suit doesn't fit anymore. I need something nice."

Sometimes that boy amazes me with his thoughtfulness. It may not be typical for most six-year-olds to ask for such a thing, but not for my son. I couldn't help but grin with pride.

Guess what he got for Christmas.

A few weeks later Bobby and I had stopped at the barbershop. He admired his new haircut and said, "Dad, I look good. I should take Mom out tonight."

"Sounds like a great idea." When we got home, Bobby and I secretly got him ready.

"Should I pay for Mom's dinner?" he asked as he put out his hand for money.

"Should I get Mom flowers?"

This was beginning to be an expensive date. "She would love that."

Bobby and I hopped back in the car and drove to our local florist. He proudly walked into the shop, held out the money I had given him on the way and announced, "My name is Bobby Perron. I'm taking my mom out to dinner because she is the best mom in the world. I want to buy her flowers. What can I get for ten dollars?"

I have never gotten so many flowers for ten dollars in my life. I called Lisa and told her to get ready. Bobby was so excited that he had a hard time sitting still. "Dad, should I open the door for Mom?"

"Absolutely." He continued asking for my advice all the way home.

I watched Bobby walk up the sidewalk to our house with arms so full of roses, he had a hard time knocking. Lisa answered and as she saw Bobby, immediately started bawling. Just before my son crawled into the car, he ran back to me. "Do you have another question, son?"

"No, Dad. I just wanted to say thank you for teaching me to be a man."

Then I cried.

I hadn't realized how much my son had learned from me. Our kids learn so much from us—some good things, some not so good. One thing's for sure; they're always watching.

EXPANDING OUR TERRITORY

From Lisa

I loved our family of five, but deep down, I longed for more children. Back when Bob and I first struggled with infertility, I felt called to adopt internationally. Since then, Bob's sister adopted a beautiful girl from China, whom we all love dearly. I was pretty sure that Bob would be open to adopting again. I also knew that international adoption was very expensive, and I was unsure how Bob would react to that.

Some days, I would weep from the ache of longing for another child. I found myself asking God again why he would put such a strong desire for a large family in my heart if it would be impossible to achieve it. One day, I felt the need to turn to the Bible. I had no idea where to begin, so I just opened it. I read the first verse that my eyes fell upon.

Fear not, for I am with you; from the east I will bring back your descendants, from the west I will gather you. I will say

to the north: Give them up! And to the south: Hold not back! Bring my sons from afar and my daughters from the ends of the earth. Everyone who is named as mine, whom I created for my glory, whom I formed and made.
Isaiah 43:5-7

I felt at peace, knowing that God would bring me my children, no matter how far from me they were born.

I kept this desire to adopt internationally in my heart for months. Around this time, the prayer of Jabez seemed to be the newest and greatest prayer. Actually, this prayer is extremely old and can be found in the Old Testament.

Jabez prayed to the God of Israel; "Oh that you may truly bless me and extend my boundaries! Help me and make me free of misfortune, without pain!" And God granted his prayer.
I Chronicles 4:10–11

I prayed that prayer every day, asking God to expand my family and if it wasn't his will to do so, to change my heart. Instead of changing my heart, he strengthened my desire. I scoured Holt International's website, the agency that Cathy and Dennis had used. I researched every country that Holt worked with and, out of all of them, I was convinced that we would find our next child in Korea.

Eventually, I convinced Bob to attend an orientation. I was ready to start the process immediately. Bob, on the other hand, wanted to take things slower. Being the provider for our family, he stressed about how we would cover the adoption expenses. Again, I prayed for Bob to have a change of heart, and if that was not God's will, then I begged for God to change mine. Every day I visited Holt's website and looked at their waiting children listing. One picture of a little boy just over a year old stood out to me. I printed his picture and placed it in a drawer by my computer.

Several times a day, I pulled out this precious picture and prayed for this little boy. If he wasn't meant to be ours, then I prayed for his forever family to be found. About a week later, Bob returned from an out-of-town ministry trip. He said, "Come here. I want to show you something."

I looked over his shoulder and watched as he logged on to Holt International's website. He maneuvered to the waiting child listing and opened a description of a waiting child—the same little boy whose picture waited in the desk drawer. As he read the description, I pulled out the picture of the same little boy. We both knew that that little boy would be our Isaiah.

We got the call six months later informing us that our son was coming home. I, along with our three children, was in Kansas at the time visiting relatives. We lived at a youth camp at the time, so Bob had to stay in Iowa. I was driving down the turnpike between Topeka and Kansas City on my way to visit my brother and his family. As soon as I heard it was someone from Holt International on the phone, I had to pull over. My whole body shook as the sweet lady gave me all of the details about Isaiah's flight that was due to arrive in Des Moines on Monday evening—only four days away. I really wish I could recall the lady's name. It seems like I should remember the one who gave me some of the most thrilling news in my life.

From Bob

It seemed like the stream of people filing out of the terminal would never end. The long anticipated plane had arrived only minutes before, and we still didn't know if our wait was over.

This flight was supposed to land at 6:30 p.m. Bad weather had delayed its arrival, causing my wife and I much distress. It was now 9:45, and we weren't even sure the passenger we awaited had made it on the plane. There was one thing of which I was sure; we would not be going home without our son.

Just when we were about to give up, a small Korean woman rounded the corner carrying whom we recognized at once to be our son Isaiah. The emotions that bubbled up in both Lisa and me can't be fully explained with words. All I knew was that for months, even if not officially, in my heart I was already his father, and Lisa, his mother.

The adorable toddler held tight to two things: his bottle and a little blue toy cell phone. There's no describing the joy we felt at that moment. The woman escorting our son handed him to Lisa and he immediately began to cry. Not just cry, he wailed and squirmed and tried everything a child his size could think of to get away.

My wife had a hard time keeping ahold of our flailing child. With a look of bewilderment, she placed him in my arms. He continued to writhe and holler. I looked around to find that there was not a dry eye in the place. Family, friends, and strangers all witnessed Isaiah's agony and our inability to comfort our own son.

Maybe if I put him down, he wouldn't be so scared. As soon as I set his feet on the floor, Isaiah ran. He fled to the only semi-familiar thing he knew—the plane.

Isaiah was quick, but thankfully my adult strides helped me to catch up with him. Lisa extended her arms, ready to have another go at consolation.

No luck. Isaiah sobbed and twisted and arched. I soon took my turn and said a silent prayer, "Please Lord, help me know how to comfort him."

That's when I noticed the escalator. I held Isaiah with his back to me, both to help him not feel threatened by facing a stranger and because it was easier to hold on to a kicking toddler that way. As soon as I stepped on the escalator, Isaiah stopped crying. The steady movement soothed him in a way Lisa and I up to that point could not. We reached the bottom.

The screaming resumed.

I ran past the elevator to the escalator going up. Again, his tears stopped. When we reached the top, I ran to the top of the other escalator and proceeded down. After a few trips up and down the escalator, I was able to turn Isaiah to face me.

My seven-year-old daughter Mackenzie followed close behind us on every trip. I hadn't realized Isaiah had noticed her until he handed her his cell phone. That simple gesture was the first time our new son interacted with anyone in our family.

On one of our trips down, I called to Lisa. "Meet me at the bottom and I'll hand him to you."

When Lisa took him, Isaiah started crying until they reached the escalator going up. After about forty-five minutes of us taking turns ascending and descending with Isaiah, we were able to put him down to play with his brother, sisters, and a few of our friend's children.

We stayed and enjoyed our new son in the airport lobby for a while before gathering him up, and after seven long months of waiting, paperwork, and preparing, we brought Isaiah Jin Tae Perron home.

In all of the years following that day, I have had a lot of time to contemplate what I learned from the experience.

On the morning of August 5, 2002, Isaiah left his Korean home with a stranger to escort him to the other side of the world. He lost everything that day: his foster parents, whom he called Eomma and Appa, his foster brother and sisters, his grandparents, his country, and his home.

He had no idea what was happening to him. Had no idea that new parents, a new brother, and sisters anxiously awaited his arrival. He didn't understand he would have new grandparents, a new country—a new home.

All he knew was his intense grief for all he lost and his tremendous fear of the unknown. He had no idea that all these things happening to him were not being done to him, but for him. It would be many years before he would be capable of comprehending that, if ever.

Have you ever experienced a point in your life where you have lost everything? Life as you knew it was over and you were lost in grief and fear.

I know I have. And just like Isaiah, I squirmed and screamed and protested as my heavenly Father tried to console me. And like Isaiah, I have tried to run back to my old life, sure that it was definitely better than what was being done to me now.

But eventually, I'd experience the peace of the escalator and accepted that ultimately, even though I didn't understand what the future held after all I had lost, there was one who knew what was best for me.

Even now, when I experience loss and confusion over what God has planned for me, I remember Isaiah playing for the first time with my other children and have hope that all will be well.

From Lisa

G oing through the adoption process this time was different than our first. The first time, Bob and I felt extreme pressure to try and prove that we would be capable parents. This time, we had three little ones to prove that we were. That didn't stop us from freaking out a bit before the home visits.

Kelsey was old enough to feel some of the same pressure during the home visits. It feels intrusive when someone comes into your home to determine whether it is sufficient enough for our new addition. The social worker tried to include Kelsey, which stressed her out a bit. She did great though, always answering the lady's questions with confidence. It put me at ease to see that the child we were raising was turning out so great.

When Isaiah first arrived home, he was very attached to his oldest sister. I was surprised to realize that it didn't bother me. I was so glad that he could be comforted. Kelsey and Isaiah still have a special relationship.

When I asked Kelsey what she remembered about Isaiah's homecoming, she said:

> Other than the train wreck that was the airport scene, life didn't really feel that crazy or altered after he came home, at least, not in any different way than a

family dynamic changes after any new baby comes home. After spending so much time waiting for him, talking about when our new brother would come home, going through the home visits and everything else, I was ready for him to be home. It was exciting and a relief to finally have him with us. Sure there was an adjustment period, but to say that life was dramatically altered for me would be disingenuous to the situation. He was my brother, and he was home. We adjusted our family to be a family of six instead of five, and life continued on, different, but more complete than before.

It's also nice now to be able to be here for him as he comes to think more about who he is and what adoption and being adopted means to him. Since we both share that experience I feel like we have been able to connect over that and just being able to listen to him try to understand his identity and how he feels about it all is something I'm glad I can help him with when he needs it and chooses to share with me. I feel like it's probably pretty normal for adoptees to have various and changing feelings on what their adoption means to them, and it's nice that he doesn't have to be alone in those thoughts since he has an older and a younger sister both adopted.

Kelsey can relate to Isaiah and Emma in a way that the of rest of us can't. We can empathize with our adopted children, but only someone who has been adopted can truly understand. I love that my adopted kids have each other in this area.

I PRAYED FOR PATIENCE

From Bob

By now, some of you are under the impression that I have a perfect family. Grant it, I do have an amazing family. I wouldn't trade or change anything about it. It's just far from perfect. We have difficulties and challenges just like every other family. One of our biggest parenting struggles comes in the form of our darling son, Isaiah.

To say Isaiah was an active child is an understatement. His doctor once described him as "a squirrel on crack." When Isaiah was five he was diagnosed with both Attention Deficit Hyperactivity Disorder (ADHD) and Oppositional Defiant Disorder (ODD). We were familiar with ADHD, but had never heard of ODD. The official definition of ODD is "the ongoing pattern of disobedient, hostile, and defiant behavior toward authority figures which goes beyond the bounds of normal childhood behavior."

That's just a fancy way of saying that Isaiah is a professional button pusher.

Let me give you an example. Isaiah was an early riser. The rest of us did not share his desire to be up before six in the morning. Every morning, Isaiah found new and creative ways of waking us up. He got in trouble every morning, but punishment was never a deterrent.

One morning, as I lay in bed, I heard Isaiah running and jumping around the house (this being his preferred method of waking everyone in the basement). I tried to ignore him, hoping Lisa would handle the situation. I'm sure she hoped the same thing about me. We both lay very still, pretending to sleep.

I heard Isaiah enter our room. I braced myself for what I knew would follow: the confrontation. Nothing could have prepared me for what happened next.

I felt Isaiah bump the side of the bed. I opened my eyes to find him holding a plunger inches from my face saying, "Smell it!"

Despite my shock, I had to give him points for creativity.

I often say, "I prayed for patience, and God gave me Isaiah to practice." I always thought I was a very tolerant person. I still feel I'm pretty laid back, but having a son that constantly challenges this side of me has taught me that I have some growing to do.

At times, while in the middle of a difficult moment, it seems impossible to find joy in the trial. But afterward, I am thankful for this challenging child.

We all face trials. It may be a conflict with a spouse or work stress. For me, a lot of my trials involved a forty-pound Korean boy. I wouldn't trade any of these experiences for anything.

From Lisa

2006

"I know you will never give me more than I can handle Lord, but right now, I am questioning your judgment!"

My five-year-old son, Isaiah, had been screaming, pounding, and kicking my bedroom door for a good twenty minutes. I had tried to make him stay in his room, but I couldn't keep him in there unless I held the door shut. I grew weary from the effort and retreated behind my locked bedroom door.

I sat with my back against the door crying. Again. I had cried more tears over this child than all of my other kids combined. At the time, I had three other children— each of them very different from the other—each of them needing a very different kind of parenting. But Isaiah was still very much a mystery to me. I had no idea how to reach him, and it broke my heart.

I cried out to God that day, "I can't do this anymore. Please show me what to do." Before Isaiah, I had confidence in my parenting. But that confidence had been wiped away. I continued to sob and complain, feeling more helpless than ever.

Then I heard God say, "I have given you everything you need to handle this. I'm not saying you have all the answers, but I have given you the ability to seek help for you and your son." That was a turning point for me. I was determined, once again, to find the answer.

Isaiah's transition into our family four years before had been difficult. When he first came home, he didn't understand the language and had no means of communication. He wasn't used to sharing time with other children, so he did whatever it took to keep the focus on himself. For the first three weeks, he communicated his discomfort the only way he knew how. He bit. Not everyone, just kids that were about the same size as him. In our house, that made our three-year-old son, Bobby, his chew toy.

At the time, I handled it the only way I knew how; I put him in time out and comforted Bobby. I didn't realize that in isolating Isaiah and giving my attention to his brother was one of the worst ways to handle the situation. It only made him grieve more.

What he needed then was comfort from me. I know that sounds backwards to those of you who have never adopted a toddler. I would've thought it was nuts before Isaiah. His lashing out was the only way of letting us know how much pain he was in.

The most difficult time to adopt a child is between the ages of fifteen and thirty-six months of age. At that age they aren't able to see that all of the change that is being thrust upon them is done *for* them and not *to* them. Isaiah was nineteen months old when he arrived in the United States. He missed his foster family. My disciplining his behavior instead of addressing that issue only made him lonelier.

Day-to-day life with Isaiah was more than a bit challenging. When he was awake, he was constantly into stuff he shouldn't be and climbing on counters, shelves, and tables. He continuously irritated his siblings, causing widespread unhappiness. I thought this would get better over time, but it didn't. Most kids, by the time they are four or five can play by themselves with little supervision. This was not the case with Isaiah. The scariest sound in the world when it came to him was no sound at all. If that was the case, he was causing trouble. I used to lie in bed in the morning thinking, "I'm not ready to do this all over again today." Every day seemed like a constant battle.

Up to this point, very few people knew how much I struggled. The only person I could vent to was Bob. I expected him to be able to fix what I could not. I was afraid if I talked to my family or friends about it, they would see it as an adoption issue and assume that I was sorry to have adopted Isaiah.

Since the first time I saw my precious boy, I have never doubted that he was meant to be mine. Isaiah was my son, I could never be sorry for that. God placed him in my heart as well as my arms. That would never change, no matter what would happen next.

I can't tell you how relieved I was to get Isaiah's diagnosis. The doctor assured me that I was not a bad mother. Anyone would feel frustrated after all this time dealing with Isaiah's disorder.

At first, I wanted the fact that we chose to medicate Isaiah to remain a secret. I had always felt (and still do) that far too many kids are medicated and felt guilty for resorting to such measures. I know now that in reality we don't medicate Isaiah to make life easier for us, although that is a positive side effect. We medicate Isaiah to make his life easier.

Relief was not immediate, but definite for all of us. All these years later, our days are no longer held hostage by Isaiah's behavior. He has learned to control his impulses better, and we have learned skills to handle him differently. Although, handling teenage Isaiah has a whole new set of challenges.

For years, I spent an excessive amount of energy trying to cram Isaiah into the mold I thought all of my children should be. No child of mine was ever going to curse or manipulate me. Not without consequences. Most of my time, I was so angry and frustrated that I couldn't get this son of mine to conform. Wasn't that my job as his mother?

Then I realized that I couldn't get Isaiah to fit the mold because he wasn't meant to. He was wired differently, and that wasn't a bad thing. It isn't my job as his mother to get him to fit my mold. It's my job to help him be molded by God.

God has taught me more through this child than anyone else. One of the most frustrating things about Isaiah's challenging behavior is that in dealing with him, it's like he holds a mirror up to me, revealing some very ugly things about myself. You can't squeeze something out of a person that wasn't there to begin with. I never knew I was capable of such anger until he drew it out. I've had to apologize to him more times than I would like to admit. But in all those moments of reconciliation, I have grown, and I am grateful.

My example of yelling and trying to control Isaiah has affected more than just him. A while back, I realized that my other children modeled my behavior. Our school day was far from peaceful. One day after hearing the reading about love in 1 Corinthians, I knew that I needed to start being a better example of what it is to be truly loving.

I printed out the verse and hung it on the wall in our dining room. We started each school day reading it and challenged ourselves to love each other better.

Love is patient; love is kind; love is not envious or boastful or arrogant or rude. It does not insist on its own way; it is not irritable or resentful; it does not rejoice in wrongdoing but rejoices in the truth. It bears all things, believes all things, hopes all things, endures all things.
1 Corinthians 13:4-6

I started with the first line, Love is patient; love is kind. That would be my first goal. The way I loved Isaiah, or anyone else for that matter, many of my days was far from patient and kind. During the day, when one of my children mistreated another, I would remind them things like "Love is not rude." or "Love doesn't insist on its own way." I had to remind myself a lot too.

Most of our days now are filled with joy and laughter, with moments of difficulty sprinkled in. Isaiah is smart and witty, and when those are used in suitable ways, he is irresistible.

He still struggles with using appropriate language when he is frustrated. When he is really upset, he tries everything to shock you. When he was much younger, for months he had tried to figure out the dreaded "f" word. He used every variation of words beginning with "f" he could think of when he was angry. I was determined not to react when he finally stumbled upon it. That is much harder than it sounds; believe me.

Isaiah's bedtime was 8:00 pm. When he was ten, he tried his best to get a later time. He tried the fairness card, but truthfully, he couldn't make it any later. He was so exhausted at night from being so active during the day, his self-control just wore out.

One night, he made it to 8:10 before I had to insist on him retiring for the night. He didn't like my decision and started to argue. I explained to him that each of his siblings had informed me a few times that he had been irritating them.

He demanded to be able to stay up later. I calmly said, "Go to bed please." His pleas to stay up got louder and he refused to comply.

Determined to remain calm, I ignored his escalating tone. I'm not going to tell you every detail of what happened next, but let's just say he crossed a line he had never dared before.

He must have seen the shift in my eyes because he immediately changed course. He testified to the injustice of going to bed before Emma, his four-year-old sister.

I no longer had ears for anything he wanted to say at that point. "Get. To. Bed. Now." I took one step toward him, and he retreated to his room.

Obviously, since I refused to bend on this issue, I wasn't understanding him. He hollered over and over, "Why are you so mad?" And, "Why won't you answer me?"

"Because right now, I am so angry with you I can't speak to you. You need to leave me alone, so I can calm down."

He didn't. I continued to clean the kitchen. He kept repeating, "Why don't you answer me?" He was like a bird pecking at my head. Peck, peck, peck. And my fury grew like a balloon filled too full. Any minute the balloon would pop and I would blow.

I finally said, "No one has ever disrespected me in the manner that you just did. It would be wise for you to leave me alone."

Silence.

Then the crying started. "I'm horrible. I don't deserve all these toys."

I thought, "That's right you don't," but said nothing.

"I don't deserve this bed, or this blanket. I'm just going to sleep on the floor."

Was this true remorse, or just manipulation?

"I don't deserve your love."

A little air released from my anger balloon.

"I don't deserve to be adopted by you. I don't deserve you and dad as parents."

Balloon leaking.

"Why don't you send me back to Korea?"

Fizzle.

How many times had I said similar things to God? How often have I felt undeserving of his blessings? His love? How many times have I wondered how God could continue to love me after I make the same mistakes, commit the same sins, over and over?

I sat in our rocker and asked Isaiah to come talk to me. I wasn't sure how to handle this but I knew I had to do something. Isaiah crawled into my lap and sobbed against my shoulder. It had to be the Holy Spirit that inspired what I said next. As I spoke the words to my son, it was as if God was speaking them to me.

"I don't love you because you deserve it. I love you because you are mine. I didn't adopt you because you deserved it. I adopted you because God meant you to be mine. There is nothing you could ever say or do that would change that. I have never thought about sending you back—just thinking of that breaks my heart."

When I first became a mother, I was shocked by the intensity of my love for my daughter—how protective I felt and how I would put her needs above my own. Until then, I couldn't even imagine how God loves.

Before Isaiah, I couldn't imagine being worthy of God's love. Now I understand that there is nothing I can do to make him love me more, and no deed too heinous to make him love me less. He loves me because I am his.

And he loves you the same.

Before Isaiah, I couldn't begin to understand that love bears all things, believes all things, hopes all things, and endures all things. I am forever grateful for the gift of this boy to illustrate love's true capacity.

EMMA COMES HOME

From Lisa

I used to ask other mothers who felt that they were finished having children how they knew that their family was complete. I wanted to know if the longing for another child was an indication that we needed to adopt again, or if it was just a feeling that I would have to get used to. God knows we had our hands full with our four kids, but still the desire to adopt again tugged at my heart. I voiced this yearning to Bob who, of course, wanted more time. The problem was that we didn't have much time. There were age limits to adopting from Korea, and Bob was months away from being too old.

We decided to look into adopting domestically through the foster care system. We attended an orientation and were discouraged from pursuing adoption this way. We felt very strongly that the new addition to our family needed to be younger than Isaiah. We didn't want to mess with the birth order. The social worker presenting at the orientation meeting said that adopting a child under the age of four through the foster system was rare. They needed couples who were willing to adopt children over the age of seven. We talked about it and resolved that this was not the way to go about expanding our family this time. We left that meeting discouraged.

A couple days later, we were perusing Holt's website—just for fun. This time we discovered our child together. We contacted Holt and six months later, we traveled to Korea to pick up our daughter.

Bob got the call from Holt this time when it was time for us to pick up Emma. It was county fair weekend, and Kelsey, Mackenzie, and I were at the fairgrounds getting their horses settled in their stalls. When he called me, I was so excited that I told everyone within hearing that we would be traveling in three days to pick up our daughter. One of the other mothers said, "You mean, you are adopting a child that you have never met?" Her reaction to my news shocked me. It was the first time that I realized how some people viewed our decision to adopt internationally. To me, picking up our daughter from Korea was no different than bringing my other daughters home from the hospitals where they were born.

It was a great trip; however, we were so overwhelmed by the whole process, we can't remember many details about being there. We met Emma the first day we were in Seoul. Despite our efforts, she wanted nothing to do with us. I was terrified that her transition would be as traumatic as Isaiah's.

The next day, I sat in the small room at the Holt International Reception Center. This day was much the same, and I was having a hard time coming up with a way to get through to Emma—the language gap being only one of our barriers.

This was the first time I had ever been out of the United States. That is, if you don't count the very brief crossing of the Niagra Falls bridge to visit a Canadian casino. (I won sixty dollars. A feat so rare for me, I feel it's worth mentioning.) Walking through the streets of Seoul and not understanding a word the people said was a stressful experience for me. On our first day in Korea, we went shopping at a Korean market place. Bob, who is always willing to try anything in cases like this, decided it was a great time to buy our children hanboks, the beautiful and colorful traditional Korean dress. I perceived the fact that we didn't speak Korean and the merchant spoke no English to be a huge problem. Bob viewed it as a challenge. If I would have been thinking clearly, I would have video taped the scene of Bob trying to gesture the various sizes and genders of our children. I'm sure you can imagine. By the time Bob negotiated a price he was exhausted.

I not only felt lost surrounded by people I didn't understand, I had a tremendous fear of getting lost and having no way of asking directions. However, by the third day in the country, we had mastered the subway system pretty well. As a back up, we had a business card to our hotel in our pocket that we could hand a cab driver and start over there if we needed.

I thought I understood the difficulty Isaiah faced when he first came home not understanding anything going on around him. I realized on our trip to Korea how frustrating it must have been for a nineteen-month-old. He not only lacked the ability to understand, but also to communicate his needs.

When Isaiah first came home, we used to sing our mealtime prayer to the tune of The Adams Family theme song. We would pound on the table with each na na.

Na na na na, (clap, clap)
Na na na na, (clap, clap)
Na na na na,
Na na na na,
Na na na na, clap, clap
We thank you for this food, Lord,
For Mom and Dad and you, Lord,

We thank you for this food, Lord,
To get us through the day.
Na na na na (clap, clap)
Na na na na, (clap, clap)
Na na na na,
Na na na na,
Na na na na,
Amen.

After about a week of this, Isaiah would come up and say, "Na na na na." when he was hungry. The first English word he spoke may have been Mama, but the first time he actually communicated something verbally was this na na na na. It may seem like a small thing, but it was a huge breakthrough.

It was a busy morning at the Holt Reception center. The lobby was filled with foster mothers and babies waiting to see the doctor for their monthly checkups. I noticed one woman with a baby on her back talking to a few people. One Holt worker was busy double-checking the Holt diaper bag sitting on the table. I recognized this bag as being one they sent with all the Holt babies when they went home to their forever families. That little boy would be going home that day. I couldn't help but imagine how excited his new family must be, anxiously awaiting his plane. I had been there.

More people gathered in our small room, and soon there were about ten people holding hands in a circle. I had read about how they gathered to pray for each child just before they went home. For at least ten minutes, they prayed. Even though I didn't understand the words, I knew that they prayed for the baby, for his birth parents, for his foster parents, and finally, his adoptive parents.

When they were finished, the foster mother tearfully handed over the child she had cared for to the couple who would be with him as he traveled to his new home. Would this boy ever know how many people cared for him? It was one of the most beautiful things I had ever witnessed.

I used to feel a lot of guilt over not traveling to pick up Isaiah. At the time, Bob and I thought it would be easiest for him to be escorted. That guilt and Isaiah's difficult transition was a great motivator in our choice to travel this time. After witnessing the prayer for that baby, my regret was replaced with great thankfulness for the people who gathered around my little boy in prayer. I believe the real reason I was in that room that day was not to see Emma, but so I could witness this baby's send off.

Language was no barrier for me that day. It was like Pentecost, when everyone was able to understand what the apostles were saying. I have always pictured each apostle speaking a different language at the same time as all of the others. I've often wondered how anyone could hear anything in that room. All those languages at once must have sounded like a bunch of gibberish. Now I wonder if the miracle wasn't that they spoke in different tongues, but that everyone understood.

Understanding goes far deeper than just hearing words. I felt what was communicated in that circle of prayer better than I would have if I had known what each person had said. Sometimes it takes the heart to truly hear.

SISTERS

From Kelsey

With Emma I was old enough to recognize the weird way people could be when you told them that you were expecting a sister, and "oh by the way, she's a toddler and from Korea." But I remember feeling that people weren't excited enough about Emma coming home. The "congratulations" seemed confused. Not everyone, to be fair, but some. And I think it's just something that some people don't know how to properly respond to, especially if they don't have adoption as a main thing in their lives, and truly, every adoption is different just like every birth is different.

We were 16 years apart, so I was quite sad that I wouldn't get to spend much time with Emma before I left the house. I felt more like an aunt to her in some ways, but I wanted to make the most of the time I had while living in the house and still try to do so whenever we are together. So like everyone else, I spoiled the crap out of her.

From Mackenzie

The Girl With the Stuffed Rabbit

A ldous Huxley once expressed: "Every man's memory is his private literature." Our happiest moments, favorite stories, and most valued life lessons are all stored in the library of our memories. From there, we can remove any recollection, dust it off, and immediately relive the most precious days of our lives. Lately, I find myself drawn to a specific section of my personal library, where I peruse the pages of the most exciting and joyful day of my life: the day I met the girl with the stuffed rabbit.

On that cherished evening, I bounded ahead of my grandparents and siblings as we moved through the Des Moines airport. My two younger brothers attempted to catch up with me, but couldn't break free of my grandmother's restrictive grasp on their hands. Far too mature to let her enthusiasm overtake her, Kelsey, alone of us children, carried herself with composure.

Once my grandfather managed to shepherd us in the proper direction and after many failed bids at freedom on Bobby and Isaiah's part, we reached the deserted waiting area. I examined my surroundings with interest, for any trip to the airport, especially one of such importance, is a novel experience for a twelve-year-old. Blindingly white paint coated the walls, and chairs upholstered with tattered blue vinyl stood in neat rows facing two escalators. Fluffy, cloud-like stuffing oozed out of the numerous tears that marred the chairs' surfaces.

Granny escorted us children to the seats while Papa poured himself some steaming coffee at a nearby refreshment station. Perched like a queen upon her throne, I goggled at the escalators. Soon, they would arrive, and the moment I had fantasized about for months would finally become a reality.

After several of the longest minutes of my life, our neighbors came to share our suspense. We speculated about when my parents' plane from Korea would land and what she would be like. Even after weeks of discussing little else, I never tired of wondering about her. This conversation only increased my anticipation, so I leaped from my seat and began to pace.

"They've landed," Papa said, forcing me to a halt.

A crowd of luggage-laden travelers filed onto the descending escalator. I scanned the throng on tiptoe, only to slouch in disappointment. My family was not among the faceless mass. In that moment, resentment toward my father's perpetual tardiness consumed me. How much longer did I have to wait?

Finally, Mom, with a small child in tow, appeared at the top of the escalator, Dad walking behind her with a video camera at the ready. The young girl, who gripped my mother's hand, seized my attention. She had short, wispy hair, dark brown in color, and wore a pink shirt with a matching skirt. Her complexion resembled melted caramel and her round face was devoid of any expression. In the crook of her arm, nestled a stuffed, pink rabbit with a green skirt, blushing cheeks, and cheerful smile.

When they reached the foot of the escalator, the child waddled forward with short, pigeon-toed strides. She had hardly managed five steps when my brothers and I flocked toward her. At our approach, she tightened her grip on the stuffed rabbit into a chokehold, eyes wide.

"Don't crowd her!" Kelsey called, but I ignored her. Nothing could keep me from where I desperately needed to be.

We surrounded the girl, kneeling in order to get a closer look. Bobby and Isaiah thrust themselves forward and pulled her into an awkward hug. I crammed my hand past the boys and brushed her arm, desperate to finally touch her in even a small way. Like Thomas the Doubter, I needed to feel the miracle before me to be certain of its reality. I devoured every detail of her petrified face with my gaze, content with watching her forever.

Mom crouched beside us, and the toddler sought refuge in her embrace, burying her face in Mom's bosom. She hid herself further from us strangers by pressing the rabbit tighter against her chest, where it acted as a familiar guardian against the sudden strangeness of her life.

As I stared, enraptured by the image before me, a fire kindled inside my chest. This blaze did not singe or burn like a forest fire, but warmed the recesses of my soul like the flames of a fireplace thaw frozen fingers after a long winter's day.

At last, I could see her. At last, I could hold her. At last, I could know her. I had thought that the monotonous months I had spent waiting and picturing the child in my mother's arms had prepared me for this, but I now knew better. Nothing could have prepared me for the moment I learned that reality is far more wonderful than imagination.

"This is Emma," Mom said, pulling away to give us a better view. "This is your sister."

NATURE OR NURTURE

The most important thing to know about our family is that even though it may have been constructed uniquely, it is like everyone else's. Our kids fight with each other like all siblings do. They also are quick to protect each other just as much as if they were biologically related.

Our family is the perfect scientific experiment in the debate over nature or nurture. Much to Kelsey's dismay, she has inherited traits from each of us. Sometimes she jokes about being glad that she didn't come from our gene pool, but for those who know us personally, it is pretty clear whose family she came from. The same thing can be said about our other adopted children as well.

There were so many funny moments in our children's growing up that we have forgotten about even though we were sure we never would. One of the things I love most about Facebook is that it provides a place for me to share funny moments as they happen. The following is a few snippets of humorous moments posted by my daughter Mackenzie or me.

Emma was talking on her toy cell phone and then asked me, "Can my boyfriend come over and have a sleep over in my bedroom?" Me, "Absolutely not."

This morning she said, "I know you said no to my boyfriend and the sleep over, but his mom said yes, and I think he is under my bed right now." Oh boy.

* * *

Playing hide and seek with Emma. Emma said, "I'm hiding in my room so don't look in there."

* * *

Me: Emma, why won't you let your brother watch a DVD in your room?

Emma: Because if he farts in there, I'll never be able to sleep in there again.

* * *

Emma: There is a bug in our house!

Isaiah: I'll get the gun.

* * *

Emma: Let's play Rock, Paper, Scissors. You be paper.

* * *

We sat in the back of church today (we arrived late). There was an adorable two-year-old playing. Emma said, "He is so cute, I'm going to take a mental picture." Using an invisible camera, she proceeded to snap away. Then she shakes it and says, "Oh man, it's out of batteries."

* * *

Emma: Bobby, Religious Ed has been canceled because of the lizard.

* * *

I rushed into the family room to take action after hearing Bobby yelling at his brother. I was relieved to find them playing Wii Star Wars III against each other and what he actually said was "GET OUT OF MY SHIP!"

* * *

Yesterday, while not receiving the respect I deserve from my lovely daughter Mackenzie, I said, "Hey I birthed you."

"You C-sectioned me. That's different."

"Only because you didn't know which way was down."

"So even in the womb I had no sense of direction!"

* * *

One day, Bobby was supposed to have cleaned the kitchen before we left home to run errands. While we were driving down the road he said, "Mackenzie doesn't know how to pump gas."

Mackenzie promptly retorted, "Bobby doesn't know how to clean the kitchen."

"That's mean!"

"Not as mean as your comment."

Bobby sighed and offered an excuse. "Well I just saw a gas pump, and it reminded me."

Mackenzie said, "Well, I just saw a bird, which reminded me of Snow White, which reminded me of Disney movies, which reminded me of Tangled, which reminded me of a frying pan, which needs to be cleaned, which of course, you didn't do.

* * *

Statuses by Mackenzie:

Emma just accused me using God's name in vain, and sent
me to my room. Apparently she thinks anytime God's name
is spoken is in vain.

* * *

Bobby is walking around with a golf club blinded folded
cause he wanted to know what it's like to be blind. So, of
course, we've been throwing things at him.

* * *

Don't know what's funnier. Emma treating her new Fur
Real dog like it's an actual puppy, or the boys acting like
it's a living, breathing carnivore that could turn on them at
any time. "Can it see us?" "It feels pain!" "Check the
instructions to see if it doesn't like boys!" Oh, the fun I
shall have with this mechanical poodle.

* * *

Emma "texting" on my phone: Dear Harry Potter, Please

come to Mackenzie's party cause she loves you, and she will prolly kiss you cause she is married to you. Don't come to Kelsey's cause Mackenzie loves you more than she does. I love you, Harry Potter, Emma.

* * *

Bobby has accused Emma's boyfriend of being pretend. I don't think this is quite fair. Granted, he does seem a bit transparent at first, but if you give him a chance he's almost too good to be true.

* * *

"Bobby! I am the music teacher and you have to do what I say! And I say you have to play piano until class is over! (Turns to me) JEESH!!! Where to we FIND these people?!!!"-Emma

* * *

Bobby kicked Emma off the piano so he could practice, so she has decided to harness all her negative emotions and write her own song. I'm not an expert on this sort of thing, but I think "'Cause He's a Girl" is a potential Grammy winner.

* * *

On our way home from Kansas City, the windshield wiper came off. Dad had to make five stops to get a replacement. He finally got lucky after forty-five minutes of searching. Bobby pointed out "You know what's funny? It stopped raining about ten minutes ago."

* * *

Emma: Hey, Mackenzie? When you were a girl like me, did you want to do ballet?

Me: Yeah.

Emma: And did you ask Daddy for a ribbon to dance with and you got it? And you loved it so much, but Isaiah broke it and you didn't love him anymore?

Me: Of course.

* * *

Emma: Sorry, I only brought one invisible Dr. Pepsi. You're gonna have to drink your spit.

* * *

My dad just read a book. I believe that is listed in Revelations as one of the signs of the apocalypse so… Goodbye 95% of the people reading this, and hello zombies.

TO THE LAND OF THEIR BIRTH

From Bob

Very few things in our lives live up to the hype that we place on them. We get ready to go to Disney World or on a cruise, and we think about it and are excited about it for months and months and months, and it comes and it goes and it was like, "Where did that go, it was so fast." The trip we took to Korea with our three youngest children was different than that. I went into the Korea trip realizing that this could be a life changing moment, especially for Isaiah, but I had no idea what kind of impact it would have on Emma. She's so sweet, and quiet, that it's hard to tell sometimes what she is thinking. The trip didn't disappoint.

From the time that I saw everybody getting off of the airplane in Seoul to the time that we got back on, it felt so right to be there and to be there with the kids. It was way to short, like every trip, but I just felt as if that moment, those moments that we were together in the land of our Korean-born children's birth, that the kids aren't going to remember every little thing we did. They're not going to remember probably that much about the hotel. They'll probably remember the buffet because it was food. But, they will remember those other moments, those moments of going to the open market, the moments of getting around in the subway, and I know without a doubt that they will never forget the moment when they got to go to Holt International and see the foster mothers that had loved them and taken care of them until they could be with us in their forever family.

I was extremely grateful. It was funny because I had arrived in Korea a few days before Lisa and the kids to lead a retreat for military families based in Seoul, however, I was still so excited about this trip, I actually went to Holt the week before just to make sure I knew how to get there, just to be sure that I had talked somebody because I was bubbling over with excitement to share this with the kids.

The day that will stand out to me though forever was the day we went to Holt with the kids. Watching Isaiah being so nervous, wondering if his foster mother would even show up, and to see his face light up when he saw her was a gift. It reminds us of the importance of love in our life. She hadn't seen him since he was nineteen months old, but it was so obvious from the minute he walked in there how much love she had for him. Without even saying a word, he felt it.

Emma is at that pre-teen stage at twelve years old; she's still trying to make sense of what happened. She gets it. She understands that the mom that was there was the only mother she knew when she was younger, but Emma didn't really know this person, so it felt a little bit weird to her to be there with her. Her sweetness showed through though throughout the whole thing. Even though she was incredibly uncomfortable with this lady touching her, she knew that it was important to her foster mother, even at her young age of twelve. She just gave her an awkward smile that, I don't think, the foster mom knew it was her awkward smile, but Lisa and I did, but Emma just hung in there, and it was really cool to see.

This was one of those weeks that will stand out for all of us as being tremendously significant for us as well as our kids. It answered questions about Isaiah and Emma's homeland, even questions that they may not have had words for. I feel so completely blessed to have been able to take this trip with them and to watch them fall in love with the land of their birth.

From Lisa

I traveled with our three youngest children to Seoul, Korea. Bob had arrived in Seoul five days previous. It was nerve wracking trying to get all of us through customs without my husband, but my prayers of a smooth entry were answered. It was chilly and rainy as we stepped out of the airport and onto Korean soil. Holt International Adoption Agency had sent a van to take us to our hotel. Our excitement to finally be in the country where our two youngest children's were born bounced around inside the van like the electricity in a plasma nebula ball that shoots lightening-like streaks when you touch it. I knew that the next four days would be some of the most significant days in the lives of not only our Korean children, but my life as well.

We were exhausted by the time we reached our hotel room, but that didn't stop us from braving the cold wind and rain and walking a few blocks for our first Korean meal: Korean barbeque. We based our restaurant choices throughout our trip on whether or not the menu had pictures of the food. Thankfully, this restaurant did. Since Bob had been in the city for a few days, he was used to not being able to understand anyone around him. For the rest of us, it was a bit unnerving. He managed to order for us with little difficulty. Along with our pork belly, we were served several side dishes. The only one I recognized was kimchi, a staple of Korean cuisine of fermented napa cabbage, Korean radishes, and spices. Kimchi was served with every meal we had in Seoul, and it was yummy.

Although the food was unique and delicious, there was one major drawback of eating in Korea: chopsticks. (I'm thinking of going on a chopsticks only diet. The sheer mental and physical energy it took me to eat each meal would surly aid me to drop a more than a few pounds.) On the last night we were there, a nice couple on the military base invited us to join them and a few other military families for authentic, homemade Korean barbeque. Much to Emma's and my relief, there were forks to eat with, so we finally were able to truly enjoy an authentic Korean meal not hindered by those two sticks.

Isaiah was outwardly excited to finally experience the Korea he'd dreamed about. Something about standing in the place that you knew that you came from, but up to this point had never experienced, has a way of completing you. His teenage years had been full of his desire to discover who he is and why he is. This trip to Korea, I think, answered some of these questions. He kept saying, "I'm home now." Part of me wanted to tell him that his home was with us, in the United States, but I think his idea of the meaning of home is different than mine. Home to him has more to do with his own identity than a place. He said that the thing that surprised him most about Korea is that the young people dressed like him in athletic clothes and Jordans and white shoes. That was fascinating to me, that the fashion sense that he has that is uniquely his here, there is rather common and very popular.

Emma, on the other hand, was more reserved. She is naturally a quiet person, so the fact that she didn't talk much about what we were seeing wasn't surprising. She observed and processed internally and took in much more than I'd thought at the time. The first time I witnessed her excitement was when we were shopping for hanboks (traditional Korean clothes) for Isaiah and her. Emma is a kid who hates to dress up. She would love to live in her leggings and big t-shirts. But when she tried on a hanbok with a beautiful full pink skirt and white satin jacket, she glowed. She smiled wide as she looked at herself in the mirror. I felt myself tearing up because for the first time, I saw how proud she is to be Korean.

Before we adopted any of our children, I remember wondering what I would feel like when my kids showed the desire to learn more about where they came from. When Kelsey was first born, I convinced myself that if she wished to meet her birthmother one day, I would support her and hoped that I would not feel threatened. After all of these years, I can honestly say that I am not only grateful for where my adopted kids came from, I would welcome any opportunity to know more about their lives before they were with me. Our trip to Korea, meeting Isaiah's and Emma's foster mothers, was a time that I will treasure. I'm so grateful for all of those who touched our children's lives before they became ours, and I am honored that God chose us to love them.

"That Felt Like A Mother's Love"

From Lisa

The first night our Korean-born son arrived home, he cried for his foster mother. Less than thirty-six hours before, he had woken up in the only home he had ever known, brought to the Holt International Adoption Services offices, handed to a stranger, and traveled around the world to be placed in our arms. He had never seen us before and had no idea what was happening. After a very stressful first introduction to our dear son, we arrived home late from the airport. Soon the family was all sleeping peacefully in their beds—all except Isaiah and me.

He was exhausted from not only the travel but also the trauma of the turn his short life had taken. I lay on the couch with him nestled against my chest. He drifted off to sleep, and my heart was bursting with love for this little human. I had almost dozed off, when he jerked awake, lifted up, looked at me, and cried, "Eomma," which means mom in Korean. He sobbed against my chest until he cried himself to sleep. Just when I thought he had settled, he jerked awake again, and when he realized who was holding him, he resumed calling for his foster mother. This happened several times that first night, and every time he collapsed crying on my chest, I cried too.

My heart broke from his sorrow. However, I also knew that he wouldn't grieve so greatly unless he had built a strong bond with his foster family and been loved immensely. I could only imagine how difficult it was for his foster mother to hand him over, and I had a strong desire to reach out and thank her for loving my son so well.

When we traveled to pick up our daughter, Emma, I was awed at the relationship between our daughter and her own foster mother. Emma pressed herself tightly against her foster mother's chest, while her foster mother spoke comforting words to her. She told her that we were her parents and that we would be taking her home with us to the United States. Even though Emma did not fully understand those words, I believe that they helped her in her transition to our family. She was not taken from her foster family; her foster family had willingly let her go, even though it broke their hearts.

While we were in Korea, we had the opportunity to meet Isaiah's foster mother, and even though we were able to thank her, the visit felt empty without Isaiah there to share it. In that meeting, both Bob and I promised ourselves that one day we would bring both Isaiah and Emma to visit their foster mothers, so they could see for themselves the women who loved them first. A few weeks ago, we fulfilled that promise.

We knew the trip to our youngest children's birth country would be emotional. At ages seventeen and twelve, we understood that, like every child these ages, our children would be wrestling with their identities. It's difficult enough to make sense of who you are when you are adopted, but add in being a different race and from a different country than the rest of your family, it's a lot to process.

We were all a little nervous when we first arrived at the offices of Holt International Adoption Services in Seoul, Korea. My husband and I had dreamed of this day, when Isaiah and Emma could come face to face with the women who had sacrificed so much for them. I couldn't wait for these ladies to see how our children had grown and to thank them for loving them so well.

As we took our shoes off and slipped our feet into the slippers provided for visitors, Isaiah said to Bob, "I'm not even sure that she's going to show up."

"She'll be here," my husband assured him, but I could tell that Isaiah was not convinced.

When we arrived at the meeting room, we were delighted to find that Isaiah's foster mother had been waiting for us. As Isaiah stepped into the room, his foster mother said in broken English, "Oh my, you so good looking!"

Isaiah sat down beside her, and they just stared at each other. Her awed expression and wide grin spoke volumes. She was overjoyed to see him again after all of these years. She said that he had cried for her when she gave him to the escort who traveled with him from Korea to the United States, and she was so heartbroken by it, she had wanted to keep him. Isaiah handed her a photo album for her to keep of him growing up in the United States, and they perused it together.

Emma's foster mother arrived a few minutes later. She'd obviously missed Emma tremendously. She held Emma's hand and gently caressed it the whole time we visited. She said through a translator that she had warring emotions. She was very grateful to us for being such great parents to Emma, but at the same time, she didn't want to have to say goodbye to our precious girl again. It wasn't until I hugged her that I felt the depth of her emotion. She held me tight as I thanked her, and she whispered her thanks to me.

A few minutes into the visit, Isaiah's foster mother presented him with a gift. She had hand written a card in Korean, and her daughter translated it into English. "You are the most precious person in the world," it read. "Don't forget this." For the first time, after all of the years of us telling Isaiah how much he was loved in Korea, he finally understood.

Inside the present were a hat, scarf, and gloves from the Winter Olympics that had been held in South Korea a few weeks before. She helped him try everything on. When he tried to put the gloves on himself, she said, "No, no," and pointed to herself. She wanted to put them on for him. It was so sweet to see her dress the boy again after all of the years they were apart.

Emma handed her foster mother the photo album we had created for her, and in turn, her foster mother pulled out a large photo album of her own filled with baby pictures of Emma that she had kept all of these years. She gave Emma a stamp with Gem Eun Ju, Emma's Korean name, spelled out in Korean in red ink. When it was time for our meeting to end, Emma's foster mother held her for a long time. She pulled back and held Emma's face in her hands and said, "Grow up well."

I hugged Isaiah's foster mother goodbye, and thanked her again for loving our son. As we got into the elevator, Isaiah said, "That felt like a mother's love."

"That's exactly what that was," I said.

Isaiah's words have since inspired me to contemplate the meaning of a mother's love. Can it even be adequately described? It's difficult to find words to describe the kind of love that I have for my children. It's easier to describe what I have observed in my own mother. A mother's love is sacrificial, unconditional, and unselfish. I'm overwhelmed by the countless times when my mother put our needs before her own. I don't think that I will ever be able to thank her as much as she deserves.

From the moment I became a mother I couldn't imagine that anyone could possibly love a person more than I loved my children. I couldn't fathom anyone loving me as much. But then I realized, like Isaiah did that day he met his foster mother, that I already had been.

A mother's love is beyond words and actions. It is a physical presence that we all carry with us throughout our lives, even after a long separation or after our own mothers are gone. I'm so very grateful for the women who mothered my children first.

ADOPTIVE SONS AND DAUGHTERS

From Bob

When I was growing up, I often thought that some day I would be a father. When Lisa and I were dating, we talked about having kids—lots of kids. I never dreamed that one day I would be an adoptive father not once, not twice, but three times. Now to be clear, I don't typically refer to my adopted children as adopted, they are just my children. I do not love them any differently than I do Mackenzie and Bobby, our homemade kids. Although I do not see my children differently, I believe I have first-hand understanding of what it means to be an adoptive father and how fiercely he loves his children.

To adopt a child is a challenging process. It typically takes months, and in some cases years. It involves home studies, lawyers, and a tremendous amount of emotional energy. When we were in the process of adopting Kelsey, it required three different lawyers in three different states and lots of paperwork.

The day of her adoption was an incredibly emotional
day. When the nurse presented Kelsey to us, I fell instantly
and completely in love. I could not stop looking at her
beautiful face. All I could think about was how much love I
felt in that moment and that I would do anything for her
and do anything to protect her. She was my child. I'm
pretty sure if anyone ever tried to harm her that would be
God calling me to prison ministry. She became completely
my responsibility that day, and my life changed forever.

Her life changed that day as well; she became part of
our family. Six weeks later, we sat in a courtroom with our
attorney as the judge made our emotional connection
legally official. Our baby became Kelsey Renee Perron.
She was legally my daughter and, at that moment, was
entitled to every legal right as any of my other children.
She would receive my inheritance. Unfortunately for her, I
have worked as a youth minister my entire life, so that
inheritance will not be that financially rewarding. But, I
pray it will be spiritually rich.

At the National Catholic Youth Conference several
years ago, I had the opportunity to speak to over 20,000
young people in Lucas Oil Stadium in Indianapolis,
Indiana. I asked the crowd, "How many of you are
adopted?" Several hundred young people and adults,
including a couple of bishops, stood up in the arena. It was

a powerful moment as this enormous crowd prayed for them. Then I read Ephesians 1:3–5.

"Blessed be the God and Father of our Lord Jesus Christ, who has blessed us in Christ with every spiritual blessing in the heavens, as he chose us in him, before the foundation of the world, to be holy and without blemish before him. In love he destined us for adoption to himself through Jesus Christ, in accord with the favor of his will."

Through our Baptism we became part of God's adopted family. I asked the audience again, how many of you are adopted, and the entire arena stood. How awesome is that. At our Baptism we live out that verse in Ephesians. Through that action, we receive God's inheritance. We become princes and princesses of the King. Our lives are changed forever.

From Lisa

For as long as the earth has been in existence, people have pondered over the reason for their being. Even if all of us can agree on the fact that God created the cosmos, for me at least, explaining the reason for my own life remains a mystery. When I was young, I thought I understood the purpose of my life. The older I get, the more I realize that God reveals his purpose for me in stages.

Discovering one's reason for being here is difficult enough for those who grow up in the family in which they are born. This task is exacerbated when one is adopted. Most of us can look to our parents or siblings and see from whom we inherited certain traits. I can say that I have my father's eyes or my mother's nose. It helps us to define who we are. An adopted person cannot do that.

First, they must question the reason they became available for adoption. I know my own adopted children have asked, "What was wrong with me?" or "Why didn't my mother want me?" We can say that adopted children are chosen or that their birthmother's actions were motivated by love and not because they didn't want their children. Unless we have experienced what it feels like to be placed for adoption by our mothers, we cannot possibly understand the complexity of feelings adopted people experience.

The first thing I think about when I contemplate adoption is how very grateful I am for the opportunity to be an adoptive mother. I used to be so jealous of those women who were able to get pregnant easily. Now, I almost feel sorry for those who never experience the miracle of adoption. I hope that my adopted children can view adoption in this way. I hope they are glad that they ended up in this family with Bob and me as parents.

I cannot talk about adoption without saying a few words about orphans. There are approximately 153 million orphans worldwide. In the United States, there are over 400 thousand children in the foster care system. Over 100 thousand of those children are available for adoption. Roughly 30 thousand children age out of the foster care system per year. These kids will never know what it's like to belong in a family. I find that heartbreaking.

God calls us all to care for orphans; however, not everyone is called to adopt. Some believe they could never adopt because it would not be natural. Others believe that instead of having biological children, the moral thing to do is to become parents of children already orphaned. Both of these groups of people ignore the fact that God designed both procreation and adoption. Both Moses and Samuel were adopted. Both were used by God to reach his lost people. Scripture mentions orphans over thirty times, and Catholic Church teaching emphasizes the necessity to care for the most vulnerable. With all of the modern day distractions, ignoring the plight of the orphan is easy. God demands Christians not only to look, but also to act. Scripture says, "Learn to do right; seek justice. Defend the cause of the fatherless; plead the case of the widow." The burning question is, how?

One of the easiest actions to take is sponsorship. Holt International has a sponsorship program that supports both families in the countries they serve and the orphans that they care for. To sponsor a child for a month costs less than a night out with your spouse. Holt tries to support the sponsored children in their birth families whenever possible. When that is not appropriate, the sponsorship dollars go to help provide high-quality care for these children while they find families for them either in their home country or internationally. If you are interested in sponsoring a child through Holt, visit HoltInternational.org.

Another way you can help is through the foster care system. You don't have to become a foster or adoptive parent to support a child in need. Bob's sister and brother-in-law, Kathy and Dan Keck, have adopted a son through the foster care system and acted as foster parents to several special needs kids. They have huge hearts for these children and are fierce defenders of the children in their care. When I asked Kathy what someone might do to help a child in foster care, she recommended several things. "You could become a mentor to a child through programs like Big Brothers Big Sisters, provide supplies for foster parents who take children in emergency situations, buy Christmas and birthday presents for kids, or provide nice bags or luggage so that kids don't have to keep their belongings in trash bags." If you are interested in helping in any of these areas, contact your local foster care agency.

More than anything, we all need to continue to pray for these children. I firmly believe that God intended for every child to grow up in a loving family.

GROWING UP ADOPTED

From Kelsey

2015

W hat's it like to be adopted?

Ah, a favorite question of mine. Who doesn't love simple questions about oneself that are increasingly difficult to answer the more you think about them? When people who have little experience with adoption (or even those that do) find out that I am adopted, this will frequently be a question that is then asked. I have twenty-five years of experience of being adopted, but I still find this question difficult to answer. I am adopted, yes, but I have also never not been adopted, so I imagine it feels somewhat similar to asking a born and bred Australian what it is like to be Australian. I could say something really cliché like, "what it's like to be adopted is to know that I am loved," and even though that's true, and I could talk about that, it's just too much and it is also a really good way of answering the question by not answering the question. There isn't one answer for this question, but I'll try to give at least one.

While I am adopted, I don't always feel adopted. I actually don't really know if I ever feel adopted. I was raised by two loving parents and boldly trail blazed the path as the oldest child (and therefore parenting guinea pig) for my subsequent four younger siblings. Other than having not been made by my parents, (a distinct gift in that I never have to accidentally visualize that, a point which I make to my siblings who must, and therefore do,) I imagine I feel just like my other siblings probably feel: reasonably put together and slightly scarred from all the times my father has complained at a restaurant. But there are times when I realize that I am adopted.

I remember the first time I realized I was adopted.

Now, let me explain, I don't remember the first time I was told I was adopted; to the best of my knowledge I have always known. I don't have any life-rocking stories of being told at some milestone birthday party, like I turn sixteen and my parents say, "Surprise! We've been lying to you!" Though that doesn't stop me from pretending that happened just to mess with those that ask. (Their faces!) No, I've always known, but that doesn't mean I always realize or remember.

I have a terrible memory. Scatterbrained with a whiplash quality of jumping subjects, I can't recall much of what I think I should. Perhaps that's normal, I don't know. But for as terrible a memory as I have, I remember the first time I realized I was adopted. I was a young child, maybe seven years old, and we were working on a class project in school about our heritage. Everyone was suppose to explain where they came from, where their ancestors hailed. Some explained that they were Irish, others German, some a true melting pot of ancestral flavors. When it came to my turn, I proudly explained that I had Native American blood coursing through my veins. Yes, that's right fellow students, I thought, I have ties to the great Pocahontas! (The Disney movie was pretty big for me.) You see, my father is 1/8 Native American, which is the same as saying he isn't Native American, but when you're little like I was, that 1/8 made me (now an even tinier fraction at 1/16) Native American.

Later that evening my mother asked me what we did in school that day. I told her about the heritage discussion and how I got to tell everyone that I was part Native American. Chuckling slightly, my mother responded,

"You're not part Native American, Kelsey."

I was so surprised she did not know that I was. How could she not? Dad was always talking about his Native

American blood quantum and I, his daughter, now proudly shared my own (infinitesimal) portion of it. There was some back and forth, which finally came to my mom informing me,

"Kelsey, you don't have any Native American blood. You're adopted."

Now I'd like to say that this was a life changing moment. That I spiraled down into a massive tangle of thoughts where I contemplated who I was and what that meant and that from that day forward I was never the same, but in all actuality none of that happened. I was seven; I was hurt and stunned but more because from that day forward I knew that I wasn't connected to Pocahontas.

As I have grown older, however, I have often remembered this little memory. It seems that we are asked surprisingly often what our family history is. Go to the doctor for anything, and you will be greeted with two double-sided pages devoted to nothing other than questions about your medical history. If you had a great-great-aunt who suffered from nosebleeds, they want to know about it. While the majority of this is pointless and unless it is something major it doesn't really matter what ailed Great-Uncle Jerry, these are two pages that I always have to skip (not complaining) because I don't know. I'm adopted.

Family lineage is a strange thing that reminds you that you're adopted. If either of my homemade siblings felt so inclined they could begin to research their family history. Connecting a line from herself to our parents, my sister could go back through the years connecting herself to countless family members that came before her, learning about where they came from, what they did, and even what ailed them, so she could better fill out those two pages in the waiting room. It is pretty amazing to think that you can look far back into the past and see the family roots of the people who would one day bring you into the world. These people are my family too, yes, but because I am adopted they are not my genealogical history. I am a transplanted branch from another tree whose only line I can fill in is my own. That is a weird feeling. I think on some level my seven-year-old self must have realized this, and maybe that is why I have remembered that moment all these years and forgotten others.

There have been other times too when I have remembered that I was adopted. When my parents are being utterly strange, as only the best of parents can be, I remember that I am adopted and think with relief about that family tree and how my genetics do not carry that particular strain of weirdness. (Sadly, nurture seems to play a part though.) Every birthday that I have, I remember that I am adopted and think how different that day was for me and the ones who brought me into the world than it was for my siblings. When I found out that my husband and I were pregnant, I was elated, but, even then in our excitement, I remembered that I was adopted, which meant that some years ago another woman, a young girl, found out that she was pregnant with a baby she did not know would become me and would come to decide to give that baby away. And when I gave birth to my daughter nine months later, and they put her in my arms, and I looked into her face, I remembered that I was adopted and thought how nearly impossible that moment must have been for my birthmother, knowing that I would not be hers.

There are a lot of things about myself that I will never know. I'll never know how to fill out those medical history forms. I'll never know how far back my family tree can be traced because, as far as blood lineage, mine is the only branch I will ever know. But being adopted does tell me one thing about myself and the family that I came from. To give your baby up for adoption has to be one of the hardest, most difficult things you can do. So while the lines will be blank and the names unknown, I know that the branches are strong.

An Interview with Isaiah

What it like being adopted?

I don't know. I just think I'm a normal kid. I've lived with you guys so long, it's hard sometimes. It's normal; you treat me the same. It's equal rights and all that.

Is there anything that sticks out to you about being adopted—any experiences that seem different because you are adopted?

People look at you different when you are with your family.

It used to happen a lot more when we lived in Iowa. People would ask questions and make comments. I think that it was because you were a lot more of a minority there. You are still somewhat here in Ohio, but you were more so there. There weren't very many Asian people where we lived. It was all very white. What's it like growing up in a white family?

Weird. Very weird. Not like in a bad way, but everyone is white, and I look very Asian, or as most people would say, Chinese.

Do you remember the first time you noticed looking different?

Nope. I don't remember. I just remember looking at myself thinking, "Man, you look good." And then I looked at you guys...

Do you remember when we told you that Emma was going to come home?

Yeah. I was excited.

What were you most excited about?

Having another Asian or not being the youngest anymore. It was exciting to hear that I wouldn't be the youngest. I didn't want to be treated like the baby. But now that I think about it, I like being treated like the baby.

When we were in Korea a few weeks ago, tell me what your first thoughts were when you first stepped outside the airport.

All of these people look attractive.

How was that? We were the ones who looked different. What was that like for you?

It was very fun because people would try and talk to me in Korean and then they would look at you guys like "Oh, white people. That's weird, we don't see much of them."

Of all the places we visited, what was your favorite?

Itewon. Because we got to get shoes and look at the street markets and all of the street food.

What did you think of the palaces?

That was really cool, very nice. The cultural things there, that was cool to see. I wish I would have worn my hanbok there because I would have gotten in free.

What about the Korean War Memorial. Did you have any thoughts about that?

Not really until we saw how thankful our tour guide was to Americans.

That was really cool. One of the things that was so cool to me was that not only was he grateful for our help but he attributed our help for enabling them to be able to other countries. They are so proud to be able to help other people in need like we helped them. And then to see all of the names of the American and Korean soldiers' names on the walls, that was very cool too.

Okay, so we've got to talk about the food. Tell me about the food, Isaiah.

The food was really nice, I liked it a lot. My favorite was probably Korean Barbeque. Kinchi is always good, but it's best in Korea.

Besides Korean Barbeque, did you have a favorite Korean meal?

Pancakes.

And the whole chopsticks thing didn't hinder you at all, did it?

Nope. I liked using them.

What did you feel when you were there?

It felt like it was home. And then we came back, and it was like back to reality.

Someday, do you want to go visit again?

Yeah.

What do you look forward to the most about going back someday?

Knowing the language a little better because I'm going to study up and learn a little Korean so I can have a conversation with people in Korea.

What advice would you give someone who was considering adoption?

Never hide it from your kid. Never hide that they are adopted. Tell them when they are young, even if they can't understand, because it will feel better to them when they are older. And tell them that you love them as much as your other kids and make them feel at home.

What were your thoughts about meeting your foster mother?

It was really nice. She was very loving. She was very kind. It was nice to see that after sixteen years, she still loved me so much. It was nice.

Would you ever consider adopting some day?

Probably. I want to adopt a kid from Haiti.

Any desire to adopt from Korea?

Yeah, I would adopt from Korea, but I'm going to have Korean kids so having a kid from Haiti would be nice.

Do you feel a stronger connection to your adopted siblings than the siblings that were born into this family?

Not really. I feel a stronger connection to my brother Bobby. We've lived with each other the longest and we shared rooms. Kelsey helped me through a lot when I had questions about being adopted, and I know that I could ask her questions anytime.

Have any of your friends ever asked you about being adopted?

They've asked if it is weird being adopted and I said, "No; it's a blessing."

Did you ever think about Korea before you knew that we were going?

Yes. Often. I wondered what it was like. Was it cool? Was it nice? And, I got to experience it, and it was very nice.

An Interview with Emma

What's it like being adopted?

Different. At school, I don't see a lot of people who are adopted like me, at least that I know. I see other Asians in my class and the other classrooms, but I don't think any of those other kids are adopted like me. They are just naturally born in their families.

How does that make you feel?

Honestly, I've never thought of it before. I just live my life how it is. There was nothing I could do about it since I was small. I guess I'm technically still small but . . .

Have your friends ever asked you about being adopted or being from Korea or anything like that?

I think my friend, I'm not going to say names, she randomly came up to me and told me, "You know, you were really lucky to be adopted," and then she just walked away.

What did you think about that?

I didn't know what to think about it. I'm just glad that she's glad that I am here.

Did you ever think about Korea before we went?

I was actually wondering a while before we even knew we were going what it would've been like if I wasn't adopted. I wouldn't have met all of these people that I've met up to today. I wouldn't have met the people that I love and care for and I wouldn't have visited all of those other places that we've visited like Disney World and Florida. Mainly Florida.

When you went to Korea, did that help you answer some of those questions?

It helped me to answer the fact that it's definitely a lot different—it's a lot different than it is here in the United States. I could tell because everybody looked the same. But here in the United States, everybody looks different. It was just a bunch of people who looked like me, and it was kind of weird.

What was it like to no longer be the minority—to have us the ones who were sticking out instead of you? When we go places here, it's obvious that you're not my biological child, so you stand out to people. What was it like not being the one standing out—that your dad and Bobby and I were the ones standing out?

To be honest, it was different. I didn't really feel different because I'm just the same person. I didn't really think about it because we were there having a good time, so I didn't really think about that. All I was thinking was, "What am I going to get?" and "What am I going to learn?" or "How much am I going to remember?" because I have a bad memory.

Was there one thing that surprised you more than anything else?

More people than I thought spoke English pretty well.

What was your favorite place you visited while we were there?

I honestly loved all of it. I didn't like the fact that I was tired most of the time because of the time difference, but I loved all of it. But if I had to pick a favorite day, I feel like it was the last day, not because I was ready to leave, but that is the day that you want to get all of your memories together and you want to treasure the last day because that's the day you'll probably remember most. The first few days I was kind of overwhelmed, and my head would be crazy because I was tired and I was wondering what was in front of me. What am I about to put in my mouth?

We need to talk about the food. What are your thoughts about Korean food?

To be honest, I don't really trust any food that I've never seen. I'll try new things, but I need to know what's in front of me. I don't want to end up putting something in my mouth and finding out that it's a bug or something. I couldn't ask you because you had no idea either. I understood the word kimchi—it looked like an onion glazed in some kind of sauce, but it did not taste like one. (It's actually fermented Kapa Cabbage and Korean radishes in a spicy sauce.)

Tell me your chopstick experience.

Let's just say that at every single restaurant, I was really hoping for a fork.

Of all of the food that we ate, what was your favorite?

Korean barbeque. The pork belly at the last place we went was so good or the pancake. I wasn't expecting that. When I think of the word pancake, I think of flour and sugar— like a batter—sweet, not something fried and crunchy.

What was your least favorite food?

(Korean food) was different, so I just didn't think much of it. If I would have stayed longer and gotten used to the taste, I think I would have liked it more. But we were only there for five days, and that was not enough time to get used to it. I really wanted a hamburger after the third day.

While we were there, we had the opportunity to meet your foster mother. What was that like for you?

It was different. It was a good experience because now I can live my life knowing that I got to meet the person who took care of me when I was a tiny baby. I also get to live my life with somebody else (me) who got to take care of me too.

I am a very interesting person in that I like touching things but I don't like being touched all that much. I'm fine being touched if I know who the person is, but she was kind of like a complete stranger to me.

To her, you weren't a stranger. But to you, she was. It's obvious that she love you greatly. Did that surprise you at all?

No, not really. I didn't expect that she would touch me so

much. I did expect her to remember me and want to hug me, but I didn't expect all of that.

Do you ever think that you would want to go visit Korea again? What would you like to do that we didn't get a chance to?

Yes. I know that I'm Catholic and all, but I would have really liked to go into the Buddist Temple when they weren't in the middle of a session. It would be cool to go inside and see their religion. I didn't want to go in there when we were there because it would be weird for them. For us, if a complete stranger walked into church during Mass and looked around, I'd be like, "Why are they taking pictures? Don't they know that we are in the middle of something?" I didn't want them to feel that way. Plus, since they look like me and I look like them, it would be even more weird.

If someone said that they were thinking about adopting, what advice would you give them? Is there anything in particular that an adopted child should know or for a parent of an adopted child to know?

Let them know why were adopted. When you think they're ready to know, you should tell them because they deserve to know, once they get old enough and start to wonder,

"Why was I adopted?"

Do you know why you were adopted? Do you still have questions?

Honestly, right now I don't feel like I need to know any more. I'm happy how I am right now.

Do you ever think that you would want to adopt your own children someday?

Yeah I would because adopting a child is really big because you're helping somebody else. There are a lot of other kids my age who don't even have a home, so it would be nice to give back.

Do you feel a stronger connection to your adopted siblings than your siblings that were born in this family?

Me and Isaiah are both adopted, we're both from Seoul, Korea, and we don't get along that much. Kelsey and Mackenzie get along great and one's adopted and one's not, so I don't think it makes a difference. They're just siblings. It's a comfort to know that I have a big sister who's adopted that I can ask questions if I have any.

GROWING UP IN AN ADOPTIVE FAMILY

From Mackenzie

In my personal experience, growing up with adopted siblings was not any different from growing up with biological siblings. It was our normal. In my mind, we are a regular family (besides, being homeschooled made us far weirder than adoption could have). My adopted siblings are just as much my siblings as my biological brother. The fact that he and I share the same risk factors for high blood pressure and diabetes does not give us some sort of special, biological bond the rest of my family cannot touch. All five of us share the bond of being part of the same family. We have the same faith, same parents, similar-enough upbringings (let's face it, parenting changed in the twelve-year gap between Emma and me), and the same Perron dysfunction.

Most of the time, Isaiah and Emma being from Korea was such a natural part of our family's makeup that it became just another thing to joke about. One time, in a fast-food restaurant (probably McDonalds, because we are proudly A-MUR-ican), nine-year-old Isaiah was getting soda from the fountain. A boy a few years younger walked up, noticed Isaiah, and asked, "Hey, do you speak English?"

Isaiah looked blankly at the boy and said, "Humyuion fjiok gagoogawah."

The boy's eyes widened like the tricycle kid in *The Incredibles* and he exclaimed, "Woah! Do you really not speak English?"

"Humfkon yong twing fdjafkjdlfjfdla."

"Wow," the boy said, a bit fazed. "That's so cool that you don't actually speak English."

As the kid walked away to join his family, Isaiah called to his retreating back, "You're alright, kid."

Growing up, I don't think I ever thought about my siblings being adopted unless someone else brought it up. Once, my family and I went to the beach with a bunch of high school campers at the camp where we grew up. My dad has always been very open about our family, using personal stories from our lives to minister to people across the country and at camp. We were pretty used to people mentioning whatever story they had heard the night before when they met us. So, it really wasn't surprising when a group of girls started asking my brothers questions while they watched a volleyball game. One of the girls turned to Bobby and said, "So, are you one of Bob's REAL kids?"

As an adult, I recognize this as a completely innocent question. She *meant* "biological," not "real," and she probably felt that my dad speaking so openly about our family gave her every right to ask personal questions. Now, I see the innocence behind her question. In the moment, however, my middle school self lacked the fully developed brain functions necessary to see anything but red. I whipped around on the bench, glared at the now startled teenager and snarled, "We are ALL Bob's real children!" Then, I stormed off in a huff, because maturity really was my defining characteristic in those days.

Using the term "real" to describe Bobby and me seemed to profane what the rest of my siblings were to me. It discounted three of the most important people in my life. I know that is not what the girl meant, and I would like to kick young-Mackenzie for being so hot-tempered and rude, but that is how I felt in the moment. My siblings are important to me, and I never want to undermine that.

Kelsey, for instance, has been the epitome of what a big sister should be. From convincing me that a parrot-ghost lived beneath my grandma's staircase (expert walkie-talkie use; 10/10) to waiting outside my window in the rain to make me quite-literally fall out of my chair when she turned around; I was treated to the full baby sister experience. When I went to college, I moved to Kirksville, Missouri, which is about twelve hours away from where my parents live. Being homeschooled my entire life in a Catholic household, the transition to a public college was jarring. Thankfully, my sister lived with her family in my dorm because her husband was the hall director. When I felt lonely, I could sneak away to play board games or spend time with my niece. When I felt challenged by morals so contrary to my own, I could escape to the basement and share my struggles with a sister who felt the exact same way. She supported and advised me when I really needed it. When I became an adult, she was right there to drastically limit the crashing and burning.

When they told me we were adopting Isaiah, I was initially very confused. With Bobby, my mom's growing stomach (that was practically unnoticeable; my mother was so fit) made the prospect of a baby brother more tangible. With Isaiah, I really did not know what to expect. I did not fully process that we were getting a new brother until I watched him carried off the plane and placed, kicking and screaming, into my mother's arms.

Though the airport was definitely a rocky start, I think we got a pretty good rapport going after a few weeks. For one, he never bit me (way to take several for the team, Bobby). For another, it really is a lot of fun having a baby brother when you are old enough to appreciate it. I loved sitting on the kitchen floor with him in my lap, feeding him from a bottle. As we grew up, there was a lot of fighting. And setting the kitchen clock forward an hour when I babysat to avoid the "Why do I have to go to bed at bedtime when Mom and Dad are gone?!" argument. And more fighting. I got a brother, not an angel after all. But, as with all brothers and sisters, he's worth having to hide the good food when I come home to visit. I love his humor, his heart, and his enthusiasm. I love watching him grow into a man.

When I heard that my parents were adopting Emma, my reaction was markedly different from when I heard about Isaiah. My mom pulled me into her bedroom and told me there was something she thought I should know, but that she wasn't ready to tell my brothers yet. She said that she and dad had decided to adopt a little girl from Korea, just like Isaiah, and, with those words, my world changed. My brain was instantly flooded with fantasies. I couldn't stop imagining the life I would live with this girl in the next few months. I would make her laugh, push her on the swing-set, and comfort her when she cried. As I paced around our house for the next hour, too thrilled to calm down, I could almost feel what it would be like to hold her in my arms. When I finally met her at the airport, waddling toward me with a stuffed, pink rabbit, she shattered my far-too-mild expectations and has continued to amaze me since.

I am thankful every day for my mom's initial infertility, which is a really weird thing to say. Who is thankful for infertility? But I am. I'm grateful for that first "No," not just because it granted me the status of "Miracle Child" (cue underrated *Joseph King of Dreams* song) a little bit down the line, but because I cannot imagine my family without my big sister. I can't imagine growing up without her as my standard to strive for. I can't imagine starting college fourteen hours away from home without her support, values, and humor two floors away. I can't imagine life without my niece and nephews who bring so much joy to everyone around them. I can't imagine how empty my life would be if Isaiah and Emma never joined our family, making us a bit more chaotic but exponentially more interesting. Our family would be pretty boring if it were just Bobby and me, and if adoption was what we needed to make our family the way it is, adoption is probably the biggest blessing I have ever known.

An Interview with Bobby

What comes to mind when you think about our adoptive family? What's it like growing up in this family not being adopted?

As far as I know, as regular as anything else. It's kind of how it's always been. I don't remember being born, so I guess that is the only difference from being adopted. Being younger than Mackenzie, I wasn't around for anyone being born; adoption is how it was.

When you look at other people's families, do you think of our as being different?

It's certainly different, just visually, but it's about the only way I can think of it being different, other than just normal family differences. We're kind of weird.

What do you remember about Isaiah coming home?

Very little. I remember the airport, that's the most of that.

Do you remember what you were thinking?

I think I was excited. I don't think I knew what was going on. I remember you gave me a Rescue Heroes toy, and I was more interested in that.

Do you remember when we told you that Emma was coming home?

I do remember that. I was pretty excited. I don't think I quite understood everything totally, but I was pretty excited about it. The time you guys spent in Korea seemed like a very long time, probably longer than it actually was. I remember doing all of that school. I don't remember the airport totally, but I do remember the drive home. I remember that Emma was not happy in the car whatsoever.

She would cry every second riding in the car unless I had my hand on her foot.

That's how it was.

You know how we celebrate Gotcha Days, what do you think of those?

I think it's important because you shouldn't just pretend that nothing is different about being adopted. It's definitely an important, special thing, and they need to know that.

When we were in our adoption prep classes, the instructor told us that we shouldn't celebrate Gotcha Day if we had biological children because that would make them feel less important or left out—that it should be called a Family Day instead. I didn't agree with them. So, I'm just curious what you thought? Did you ever feel like, "I don't get a Gotcha Day."

My Gotcha Day was my birthday.

What are your thoughts about your dad and I writing this book?

I'm excited to see the story written out because we had the other book, *Lessons Learned from a God-sized Family*, which was cool seeing our stories written down, but I think having a more in depth accounting is good, and I think it will be interesting to see.

A lot of people might wonder whether you felt a stronger bond with your biological sister than your adopted siblings.

I don't think so, no. It's just no different—her being biologically related to me—because we grew up all together and we were all siblings, so it doesn't make any difference.

If you were to talk to anyone who were thinking about adoption but were concerned about their biological children, what advice would you give them?

Don't worry about it so much and don't try to treat it like it's something weird. If you treat it like it's normal, that it's going to be their life, then they're not going to have issues with it.

When we are in public and people are taking special notice of our family, how does that make you feel? Or have your friends ever asked you about that?

Honestly, I don't really notice when people react to the fact that Isaiah and Emma, at least, don't quite look like the rest of the family. I don't notice, but that might be that I don't pay attention. People don't normally ask too many questions. There's never a rude amount of questions.

So do you think you might ever consider adopting someday?

I don't know, maybe. I'll just have to see where life takes me. I'm a bit young to say, "Yeah," now. I don't even know what I'll be doing in ten years. I wouldn't be opposed to it.

QUESTIONS TO ~~NEVER~~ ASK
ADOPTED FAMILIES

We've all seen our share of lists. You know the ones—the ones that begin with something like, "Ten Things to Never Say to" fill in the blank with whatever circumstance that applies to a particular situation like people dealing with infertility, or depression, or disorders, or kittens, or big fat noses or whatever. As a matter of fact, I considered having such a list in this book. However, my oldest daughter discouraged me from this.

Kelsey reminded me that people have been created to have a curiosity about situations that they have not experienced. It is natural to ask questions. She said, "An improperly worded question isn't that big of a deal. It doesn't offend me and it shouldn't offend you (the you in the general sense, which I suppose would also include you)." She was right. If we take offense to what might seem like someone's nosiness, we lose the opportunity to educate. Kelsey said, "Making someone feel like they shouldn't ask this takes away our opportunity to voice and explain just how loving and open the heart can be. And we need to remember too, as adoptive families, that not everyone is called to adopt, and they might think we're crazy, and THAT'S OKAY TOO. Besides, you kind of have to be crazy to adopt." The reality is that I love to speak about the miracle of adoption, so I shouldn't be discouraging anyone's God-given curiosity.

After Isaiah came home, it seemed we couldn't go anywhere without being bombarded with questions. One day, Kelsey, Isaiah, and I went to Walmart. As we waited in the checkout line, I noticed the cashier kept looking first at Isaiah sitting in the cart and then at Kelsey and me. I knew her thoughts; I just wasn't sure if she would voice them. When it became our turn, she asked the same question that we were asked every time we ventured into public.

"Is he adopted?"

Without missing a beat, Kelsey said, "No, but he does look an awful lot like the mailman."

While it was pretty funny at the time, I probably should have been more kind to the woman and answered her myself. Hearing the same questions or comments over and over can get tiresome, but that is no excuse.

So, taking Kelsey's advice, instead of a list of forbidden questions, I listed three commonly asked questions or comments about adoption and how I should respond:

1.   Is it difficult to love a child that isn't your own or share your biology?

At first glance, this question seems rude. However, I am sure that many people have had the urge to ask the same question. The answer is no. It is not difficult because he or she is mine. My ability to love my adopted children has nothing to do with whether or not they came from my own body. I honestly believe that God places in the hearts of adoptive parents maternal or paternal love for whom he has placed in their care.

Most of us have had a similar experience. Have you ever had a friend that has felt more like family? You love them like a brother or sister and would do anything to help them as if they were actually family. The truth is they are. We are all part of the same family.

2.   They are so lucky that you have saved them from..."

I have often said to this comment that I am the lucky one, and I truly feel that way. I hope all of my kids feel lucky, not because Bob and I have saved them, but because they are loved tremendously, whether they are our adopted or homemade children. It is also important to remember that every adopted child's story begins with a tragedy. Kelsey said, "As an adopted child, I can say, personally, that I wish we could live in the perfect world where no child would ever need to be adopted and could be raised by their biological mother and father in a happy home under perfect circumstances." We live in an imperfect world run by imperfect people who make imperfect decisions. Nonetheless, we are loved perfectly by our perfect God who brings together families of all kinds to love each other.

3. What about her real mother?

This one is the most difficult one to address for me emotionally. My first instinct is to snap that I am her real mother. However, the question is a legitimate one. It is extremely difficult to comprehend how a mother could place her child for adoption. I wondered that too when I was in high school. But then a girl who, like me, wanted a lot of children, surprisingly placed her newborn son for adoption. It was the most difficult, loving, and unselfish thing she had ever done. She didn't want to lose her child, but she knew that she was not in a position to raise him well. Yet.

To this comment, Kelsey said, "I realize this one is probably a trigger for any adoptive mom. But guess what, it also can be a trigger for adopted kids. This question does not offend me. I want people to feel confident to ask this so that I can explain the difference between my birthmother and my mother."

The person making this comment isn't intending to disregard my motherhood. So what about her real mother? Her birthmother was a scared young woman who had the strength to first give her baby life and second to make the most difficult choice a mother ever has to make. So please, pray for her and the birthmothers of my other children.

I encourage anyone who has genuine questions about adoption to ask them. Some may want to talk about adoption as part of their own discernment process. Others may just simply be curious. The motivation doesn't matter. I want everyone to know the beauty and miracle of adoption. That can't happen if we take offense to the questions. However, it is extremely important when asking such questions that you are sensitive to the fact that not every adopted child is comfortable with discussing his or her personal adoption story with strangers. Many of the difficulties they face when it comes to their own adoptions are personal, and they have every right to keep these difficulties to themselves.

GRATEFUL

From Lisa

Tonight as I sit and ponder our adoption journey, I am filled with emotion. Our road was filled with tremendous sorrow and even greater joy. I shake my head at my extreme lack of faith and marvel at the generosity of a God that I turned away from on numerous occasions. Even when I wasn't capable of loving him, he loved me. I was so undeserving, but I suppose we all are.

When we look at our children, we don't see adopted or biological. They are all our children. We love them all the same no matter how they came to us. However, just because I never think about my adopted children differently, it doesn't mean that my adopted children never feel that way. The loss of biologic connection and, for two of my children, the country of their birth, is real. I read once that "one of the most sacrificial acts of love adoptive parents can do is to give up their preconceptions and agendas about what their child's views should be and be open to hear the conflicting emotions and thoughts their child often experiences." (Sherrie Eldridge, *Twenty Things Adopted Kids Wished Their Adoptive Parents Knew*). I would love to be everything my kids need in a parent, but the fact is that I can't—not even for the two I birthed. All I can do is pray that God will give me the wisdom to love and support them the way they need me to.

Our three oldest children are grown now. Kelsey married an amazing man who cherishes her and their children. Adam and Kelsey have given us four of the cutest and smartest grandchildren on the planet. It brings me great joy to see their family grow as rapidly as I had wanted mine to grow. Had that been the case for me, I wouldn't have any of these people in my life.

Most of us have heard the saying, "The best part about grandchildren is that I get to spoil them and send them home." I say the best thing about grandchildren is when you first witness seeing your child experience the same maternal love for her children as you have for her.

Mackenzie earned her master's degree in education and is starting her career as an elementary teacher this year. Bobby will be joining the Air Force in a few short months. Isaiah will graduate next year. Thankfully, we still have a few years with Emma at home with us.

It's amazing how when all of the kids were home and we were often overwhelmed with surviving the days, we had no idea how quickly the time would pass. I couldn't imagine what it would be like when they all were grown. So far, by the grace of God, our kids have turned out pretty great.

I am so grateful that God said no to our idea of building our family. His yes was so much greater.

ABOUT THE AUTHORS

Bob and Lisa Perron have been married for over thirty years. Bob speaks nationally and internationally at parish missions, men's conferences, and marriage retreats. Lisa is the author of the fiction novel entitled *Among the Reeds*. Together, they are interested in adopting her baby interested in adopting her baby starting a new ministry to support couples who have struggled with infertility, are considering adoption, or those who have adopted. Three of their children are grown. They live in Ohio with their two youngest children.

www.ingramcontent.com/pod-product-compliance
Lightning Source LLC
LaVergne TN
LVHW051404080426
835508LV00022B/2968